PANJSURAH
SHAREEF

(A Collection of **Sixteen Surahs**
from The Holy Qur'ãn)

Transliteration in Roman Script
by **M.A. Haleem Eliasi**
with Original 'Arabic Text

English Translation by

Abdullah Yusuf Ali

New Delhi-110006 (India)

KITAB BHAVAN

Publishers, Distributors, Exporters & Importers
1784, Kalan Mahal, Darya Ganj,
New Delhi - 1100 02 (India)

Phones : (91-11) 23277392/93, 23274686, 32906494
Fax   : (91-11) 23263383

Website: www.nusratalinasri.com

Email   : nasri@vsnl.com
        : nusrat@bol.net.in

First Edition   : 2002
3rd Edition   : 2014

ISBN   : 81-7151-299-2
Book Code No.   : P00018

Printed & Published in India by :
Nusrat Ali Nasri for KITAB BHAVAN
1784, Kalan Mahal, Darya Ganj,
New Delhi - 1100 02 [India]

CONTENTS

KEY TO TRANSLITERATION

In this transliteration Signs of Interrogation, Interjection, Quotation Marks, and Dashes have been introduced for clarification of intonation and meaning. Gunna = n (nasal sound) as in uncle. This occurs about 70% in the Qur-'aan. For مَد elongation of vowels three symbols have been introduced :

a, i, u, as in بَ = ba بَا = baa بَآ = baaa بِ = bi بِى = bii تَى = biii بُ = bu بُوْ = buu بُوَ = buuu

All these, I believe, are innovations.

There is only 'Ma'-ruuf' sound in the Qur-'aan as بِ = bi بُ = bu.

There is no 'Majhuul' sound in the Qur-'aan except in one word: مَجر يها

'Majraihaa' (as in 'ray') (S. XLI. 11).

Signs of Pause in the Arabic Text

1. (these are most important)   ط ـ م ـ سكته ـ ه ـ o ـ ؤ

2. (preferable) وقفه

3. (not preferable) لا

4. (permissible)   صل ـ نے ـ طے ـ ق ـ ز ـ ر ـ ج

5. (preferable) وقف منزل ـ وقف غفران ـ وقف جبريل ـ وقف النبى ـ وقف كفران ـ وقف

6. (permissible)   ص ـ ﮦ ـ o

7. ∴ ∴ The pause between two groups each of three dots is to be connected either with the preceding text or the subsequent text. It is not to be detached from either.

ALPHABETS

ء (hamza) = ٔ (apostrophe) ب = b ت = t (as 'th' is pronounced in 'bath') ث = s̤ ج = j ح = ḥ

خ = kh د = d (as 'th' in 'thou-thee') ذ = z̤ ر = r ز = z س = s (as in sir-sister) ش = sh ص = ş

ض = z̤ ط = ţ ظ = z̤ ع = ' (inverted apostrophe) غ = g ف = f ق = q ك = k ل = l م = m

ن = n غُنَة (gunna) = n̄ (nasal sound as 'n' is pronounced in uncle) ه or ﮦ = h و = w ى = y.

ا (Alif) is not be confused with ء (hamza). If it has diacritical marks (as ◌َ ـ ◌ِ ـ ◌ُ ـ ◌ٌ ـ ◌ً) it is hamza. Alif is always followed by another letter as ب = ba با = baa.

The seven groups of ʿArabic letters which closely resemble in pronunciation are given below where the first letter is basic.

(1) ء (همزه) = ʿ = ع = ʿ (2) ت = t = ط = ṭ = ه = h = ح = ḥ (4) س = s = ص = ş = ث = ş (5) ز = z

ذ = z = ض = ẓ = ظ = ẓ = ج = j (6) ك = k = ق = q = خ = kh (7) ن = n غُنّه (gunna) = ñ

ء = ʾu or أُ = ʾu ء = ʾiii or اِىٓ = ʾiii ء = ʾaaa or آ = ʾaa ء = ʾaa or أُ = ʾa or اِ = ʾa

or اُوْ = ʾuu or اُوْ = ʾuu بُوْ = buu بُ = bu بِىٓ = biii بِىٓ = bii بِنى = bi بَآ = baaa بَا = baa بَ = ba

بُوّ = buuu عَا or عَ = ʿaa عَآ = ʿaaa عِ = ʿi عِىٓ = ʿii عِىٓ = ʿiii عُ = ʿu عُوْ = ʿuu عُوّ = buuu

ه or هُ = hu هَىٓ = hiii هِىٓ = hii ه or هِ = hi هَآ = haaa هَآ = haa هَا = ha ة or هَ = ha or هَ uuu

هُوّ = huuu ى = ya يَا = yaa يَآ = yaaa ى = yi ىِ = yii يَىٓ or يْىٓ = yiii and so on. ب = ba

بَىٓ = bay (as in by). أَ = ʾa أَىٓ = ʾay كَ = ka كَىٓ = kay شَ = sha شَىٓ = shay يَىٓ = yay and so

on. بَ = ba بَوْ = baw (as in now) مَ = ma مَوْ = maw عَوْ = ʿaw أَوْ = ʾaw اِوْ = ʾiw أُوّ = ʾuwwa

بِ = bi بِىَ = biy بِىَ = biyyi أَىَ = ʾay أَىُّ = ʾayyu بُىُّ = buyyu وَوْ = waw بُىَّ = biyyu بُوَّ = buwwa

أَنْ or أُ = ʾan اِنْ or اِ = ʾin أُنْ or أُ = ʾun بَنْ = ban بِنْ = bin بُنْ = bun بَآ = baa بَعْ = baʿ

أَءِ = ʾa آغْ = ʾa بِنى = biʾ بُوْ = buʾ يُوْ = yuʾ مُوْ = muʾ أَبّ = ʾabba اللّٰه = ʾAllaahu مَ or مَا = maa

وَمَوْرُ or و = wuu لَ = la لآ = laa لآ = laaa اِقْرَءْ = ʾiqra يَااَيُّهَا اْلاِ نْسَانُ = yaaa-ʾayyu-hal-ʾiñsaanu

اِذَا = ʾizaa يَقَوْم = yaa-qawmi قُل اللّٰهُمَّ = Qulilla-humma حَتّى = ḥattaa حَجّ = Ḥajj للّٰه = lillahi

فِرعَوْنُ = Fir-ʿawnu قَدّتْ = qatta أَنْ رَّ = ʾalla مِنْ رَّ = mirra لُقّكَ = lukka لَتّ دَّ = ladda اللّٰه =

وَيْلٌ يَّوْ مَنِذِ = ʾaal-laahu وَالضّآ لَيِنْ = wa lazzaaal-liiin نُوْحُ ابنه = Nuuḥu-nibnahuu

way-luñy-Yawma-ʾizin أَعْلَمُ = ʾa-lamu اِلَيْكُمْ = ʾilay-kum اخِرَةُ = ʾAakhi-ratu قُرْاٰنُ = Qur-ʾaanu

اَضْغَاثُ = ʾaz-gaaşu كِتَابُ = Kitaabu اٰدَمُ = ʾAadamu قَيُّوْمُ = Qayyuumu وُرِّى = wuuriya

فِى اْلاُمِّيْنَ = fil-ʾummiy-yiina

Gunna occurs before ب ت ث ج د ذ ز س ش ص ض ط ظ ف ق ك م ن و ى=

b t ş j d z ẓ s sh ş ẓ ṭ ẓ f q k m n w y, e.g. أَنْتَ = ʾañta أَنْزَ = ʾanza أَنْكَ = ʾanka and so on.

مَنْ ىَّ = mañyya أَنْ ىَّ = ʾañyya أُنْ وَّ = ʾuñwwa اِنْ وَّ = ʾiñwwa طَنْ وَّ = ʾañwwa

مِنْ وَّال = miñw-waal مَنْيَّشَآءْ = mañy-yashaaa.

But when silent ن = n is followed by ب = b, ن is pronounced like م = m with a gunna: e.g. اَنْبَا = 'ambaa.

When there is silent م = m followed by another م = m, or silent n followed by another n, there is automatically a gunna (nasal sound) between the two and it is genereally pronounced.

Therefore we have avoided gunna, e.g. عَمَّ = `amma   اَنَّ = 'anna   اِنَّ = 'inna   لَيْسَ = laysa   بَيْنَ = bay-na   عَلى = `alaa   زُ يَنَ = zuyyina   صَوْمٌ = Şawm   قَوْمٌ يَعْقِلُونْ = Qaw - muñy-ya`- qiluun   اِلى = 'ilaa   عَلَيْكَ = `alayka   اَللّهُمَّ صَلَّ على سَيِّدِنَامُحَمَّدٍ وَ بَارِكْ وَسَلِّمْ = 'Allaahumma şalli `alaa Sayyi-dinaa Muḥammadinw-wa baarik wa sallim.   رَآ = ra-`aa   جَآءَ = jaaa-'a   ءَ اَنْتُمُْ = 'a-'antum   دَيْنٍ = dayn   قُلْ = Qul   قَالَ = qaala   اَلَّذِى = 'allazii   سَمَآءُ = samaaa-'u   اَهْلَلْ = 'ahlal   بِسْمِ اللّٰهِ الرّحْمنِ الرّحِيْمِ = Bismillaa-hir-Raḥmaanir-Raḥiim.   اَعُوْذُ = 'a-`uuzu   يٰبَنِيْ اِسْرَ آئِيْلَ = Yaa-Baniii-'Is-raaa-'iila   هَدْىْ = hady   حَىَّ = ḥayy   اَرْسَلَ = 'arsala   يَوْمُ = yamu   مُحَمَّدٌرَسُوْلُ اللّٰهِ = Muḥammadur-Rasuu-lullaah   لآ اِلهَ اِلاَّ اللّٰهُ = Laaa 'ilaaha 'il-lal-laah   طَانَا 'ana   اَسْ = `as   قِيَامَةٌ = Qiyaamah   اِيَّاكَ = 'iyyaaka   حَيْثُ = ḥay-şu   كَيْفَ = kayfa   اَشْهَدُ = 'ash-hadu   غَيْرْ = gay-ra   يَدَيْهِ = yaday-hi   رُ ئْيَا = ru-'yaa   اَرَءَيْتُمْ = 'ara-'ay-tum   يَسْ = yas   اُسْ = 'us   اِسْ = 'is   اَلَيْنْكَ = ma'-waa   مَاوَى = ma'-waa   هؤُ لآءِ = haaa-'ulaaa-'i   هُوَالَّذِىْ = Hu-wallazii   اٰمَنُوْا = 'aamanuu   مَعَكُمْ = ma-'akum   اُلآءِكَ = 'ulaaa-'ika   يَسْئَلُوْنَ = yas-'aluuna   لِى = liya   يآ اَيُّهَا النَّبِيُّ = yaaa-'ayuu-han-nabiyyu   اَبْرَاهِيْمُ = 'Ibraa - hiimu   صَلوةٌ = Şalaatun

Verses 83–Sections 5

Bismillaahir-Rahmaanir-Rahiim.

1. Yaa-Siiin.

2. Wal-Qur-'aanil-Hakiim,-

3. 'Innaka la-minal-mursaliin,

4. 'Alaa Siraatim-Musta-qiim.

5. Tañziilal-'Aziizir-Rahiim,

6. Li-tuñzira qawmam-maaa 'uñzira 'aabaaa-'uhum fahum gaafiluun.

7. Laqad haqqal-Qawlu 'alaaa 'aksarihim fahum laa yu'-minuun.

8. 'Innaa ja-'alnaa fiii 'a'-naaqihim 'aglaalañ fahiya 'ilal-'azqaani fahum-muqmahuun.

Yā-Sîn (being Abbreviated Letters)

In the name of Allah, Most Gracious, Most Merciful.

1. Yā Seen.
2. By the Qur'ān, full of Wisdom,—
3. Thou art indeed one of the messengers,
4. On a Straight Way.
5. (It is a Revelation) sent down by (Him), the Exalted in Might, Most Merciful,
6. In order that thou mayest warn a people, whose fathers were not warned, and who therefore remain heedless (of the Signs of Allah).
7. The Word is proved true against the greater part of them: for they do not believe.
8. We have put yokes round their necks right up to their chins, so that they cannot bow their heads.

9. Wa ja-'alnaa mim-bayni 'aydiihim saddañwwa min khàlfihim saddañ-fa-'agshay-naahum fahum laa yubsiruun.

10. Wa sawaaa-'un 'alayhim 'a-'añzartahum 'an lam tuñzir-hum laa yu'-minuun.

11. 'Innamaa tuñziru manittaba-'az-Zikra wa khashiyar-Rahmaana bil-gayb: fabash-shirhu bi-Magfiratiñwwa 'Ajriñ-Kariim.

12. 'Innaa Nahnu nuhyil-mawtaa wa naktubu maa qaddamuu wa 'aasaarahum: wa kulla shay-'in 'ah-saynaahu fiii 'Imaamim-mubiin. (Section 2)

13. Wazrib lahum-masalan 'As-haabal-Qaryah. 'Iz jaaa-'ahal-mursaluun.

---

9. And We have put a bar in front of them and a bar behind them, and further, We have covered them up; so that they cannot see.

10. The same is to them whether thou admonish them or thou do not admonish them: they will not believe.

11. Thou canst but admonish such a one as follows the Message and fears the Most Gracious, unseen: give such a one, therefore, good tidings, of Forgiveness and a Reward most generous.

12. Verily We shall give life to the dead, and We record that which they send before and that which they leave behind, and of all things have We taken account. In a clear Book (of evidence).

13. Set forth to them, by way of a parable, the (story of) the Companions of the City. Behold, there came messengers to it.

14. 'Iz 'arsalnaaa 'ilayhimus-nayni fakazzabuuhumaa fa-'azzaznaa bi-saalisin-faqaaluuu 'innaaa 'ilaykum-mursaluun.

اِذْ اَرْسَلْنَآ اِلَيْهِمُ اثْنَيْنِ فَكَذَّبُوْهُمَا فَعَزَّزْنَا بِثَالِثٍ فَقَالُوْٓا اِنَّآ اِلَيْكُمْ مُّرْسَلُوْنَ ۝

15. Qaaluu maaa 'antum 'illaa basharum-mislunaa wa maaa 'anzalar-Rahmaanu min-shay-'in 'in 'antum 'illaa takzibuun.

قَالُوْا مَآ اَنْتُمْ اِلَّا بَشَرٌ مِّثْلُنَا ۙ وَمَآ اَنْزَلَ الرَّحْمٰنُ مِنْ شَيْءٍ ۙ اِنْ اَنْتُمْ اِلَّا تَكْذِبُوْنَ ۝

16. Qaaluu Rabbunaa ya'-lamu 'innaaa 'ilaykum la-mursaluun:

قَالُوْا رَبُّنَا يَعْلَمُ اِنَّآ اِلَيْكُمْ لَمُرْسَلُوْنَ ۝

17. Wa maa 'alaynaaa 'illal-Balaagul-mubiin.

وَمَا عَلَيْنَآ اِلَّا الْبَلٰغُ الْمُبِيْنُ ۝

18. Qaaluuu 'innaa tatayyarnaa bi-kum: la-'illam tantahuu lanar-jumannakum wa laya-massannakum-minnaa 'azaabun 'aliim.

قَالُوْٓا اِنَّا تَطَيَّرْنَا بِكُمْ ۚ لَئِنْ لَّمْ تَنْتَهُوْا لَنَرْجُمَنَّكُمْ وَلَيَمَسَّنَّكُمْ مِّنَّا عَذَابٌ اَلِيْمٌ ۝

19. Qaaluu taaa-'irukum-ma-'akum: 'a-'in zukkirtum? Bal 'antum qawmum-musrifuun !

قَالُوْا طَآئِرُكُمْ مَّعَكُمْ ۚ اَئِنْ ذُكِّرْتُمْ ۚ بَلْ اَنْتُمْ قَوْمٌ مُّسْرِفُوْنَ ۝

20. Wa jaaa-'a min 'aqsal-Madiinati rajuluny-yas-'aa qaala yaa-qawmittabi-'ul-mursaliin:

وَجَآءَ مِنْ اَقْصَا الْمَدِيْنَةِ رَجُلٌ يَّسْعٰى ۖ قَالَ يٰقَوْمِ اتَّبِعُوا الْمُرْسَلِيْنَ ۝

---

14. When We (first) sent to them two messengers, they rejected them: but We strengthened them with a third: they said, "Truly, we have been sent on a mission to you."

15. The (people) said: "Ye are only men like ourselves; and The Most Gracious sends no sort of revelation: ye do nothing but lie."

16. They said: "Our Lord doth know that we have been sent on a mission to you:

17. "And our duty is only to deliver the clear Message."

18. The (people) said: "For us, we augur an evil omen from you: if ye desist not, we will certainly stone you, and a grievous punishment indeed will be inflicted on you by us."

19. They said: "Your evil omens are with yourselves: (Deem ye this an evil omen). If ye are admonished? Nay, but ye are a people transgressing all bounds!"

20. Then there came running, from the farthest part of the City, a man, saying, "O my People! obey the messengers:

21. 'Ittabi-'uu mallaa yas-'alukum 'ajranwwa hum-muhtaduun. (PART–23)

22. **WA MAA LIYA** laaa 'a-budullazii fataranii wa 'ilayhi turja-'uun.

23. 'A-'attakhizu miñ-duunihiii 'aalihatan 'iñy-yuridnir-Rahmaanu bizurril-laa tugni 'annii shafaa-'atuhum shay-'añwwa laa yuñqizuun.

24. 'Inniii 'izal-lafii Zalaalim-mubiin.

25. 'Inniii 'aamantu bi-Rabbikum fasma-'uun !

26. Qiilad-khulil-Jannah. Qaala yaa-layta Qawmii ya'-la-muun,

27. Bimaa gafara lii Rabbii wa ja-'alanii minal-mukramiin !

28. Wa maaa 'añzalnaa 'alaa Qawmihii mim-ba'-dihii min juñdim-miñassamaaa-'i wa maa kunnaa muñziliin.

---

21. "Obey those who ask no reward of you (for themselves), and who are themselves guided.

22. "Why should not I serve Him Who created me, and to Whom ye shall (all) be brought back.

23. "Shall I take (other) gods besides Him? If The Most Gracious should intend some adversity for me, of no use whatever will be their intercession for me, nor can they deliver me.

24. "I would indeed, then be in manifest Error.

25. "For me, I have faith in the Lord of you (all): listen, then, to me!"

26. It was said: "Enter thou the Garden." He said: "Ah me! Would that my People knew (what I know)!

27. "From That my Lord has granted me Forgiveness and has enrolled me among those held in honour!"

28. And We sent not down against his People, after him, any hosts from heaven, nor was it needful for Us so to do.

29. 'Iñ kaanat 'illaa ṣayḥatañw waahidatañ-fa-'izaa hum khaamiduun.

اِنْ كَانَتْ اِلَّا صَيْحَةً وَّاحِدَةً فَاِذَا هُمْ خَامِدُوْنَ ۝

30. Yaa-ḥasratan 'alal-'ibaad! Maa ya'-tiihim-mir-rasuulin 'illaa kaanuu bihii yastahzi-'uun !

يٰحَسْرَةً عَلَى الْعِبَادِ مَا يَاْتِيْهِمْ مِّنْ رَّسُوْلٍ اِلَّا كَانُوْا بِهٖ يَسْتَهْزِءُوْنَ ۝

31. 'Alam yaraw kam 'ahlaknaa qablahum-minal-quruuni 'annahum 'ilayhim laa yarji-'uun?

اَلَمْ يَرَوْا كَمْ اَهْلَكْنَا قَبْلَهُمْ مِّنَ الْقُرُوْنِ اَنَّهُمْ اِلَيْهِمْ لَا يَرْجِعُوْنَ ۝

32. Wa 'iñ kullul-lammaa jamii-'ul-ladaynaa muhzaruun. (Section 3)

وَاِنْ كُلٌّ لَّمَّا جَمِيْعٌ لَّدَيْنَا مُحْضَرُوْنَ ۝

33. Wa 'Aayatul-lahumul-'arzul-maytah: 'ahyaynaahaa wa 'akhrajnaa minhaa ḥabbañ faminhu ya'-kuluun.

وَاٰيَةٌ لَّهُمُ الْاَرْضُ الْمَيْتَةُ اَحْيَيْنٰهَا وَاَخْرَجْنَا مِنْهَا حَبًّا فَمِنْهُ يَاْكُلُوْنَ ۝

34. Wa ja-'alnaa fiihaa jannaatim-min-nakhiiliñw-wa 'a'naa-binw-wa fajjarnaa fiihaa minal-'uyuun:

وَجَعَلْنَا فِيْهَا جَنّٰتٍ مِّنْ نَّخِيْلٍ وَّاَعْنَابٍ وَّفَجَّرْنَا فِيْهَا مِنَ الْعُيُوْنِ ۝

35. Liya'-kuluu miñ samarihii, wa maa 'amilat-hu 'aydiihim: 'afalaa yash-kuruun?

لِيَاْكُلُوْا مِنْ ثَمَرِهٖ وَمَا عَمِلَتْهُ اَيْدِيْهِمْ اَفَلَا يَشْكُرُوْنَ ۝

---

29. It was no more than a single mighty Blast, and behold! they were (like ashes) quenched and silent.
30. Ah! alas for the servants! there comes not a messenger to them but they mock him!
31. See they not how many generations before them We destroyed? Not to them will they return:
32. But each one of them all—will be brought before Us (for judgment).
33. A Sign for them is the earth that is dead: We do give it life, and produce grain therefrom, of which ye do eat.
34. And We produce therein orchards with date-palms and vines, and We cause springs to gush forth therein:
35. That they may enjoy the fruits of this (artistry): it was not their hands that made this: will they not then give thanks?

36. Subhaanallazii khalaqal-'azwaaja kullahaa mimmaa tumbitul-'arzu wa min 'anfusihim wa mimmaa laa ya'-lamuun.

37. Wa 'Aayatul-lahumul-Laylu naslakhu minhun-Nahaara fa-'izaa hum-muzlimuun;

38. Wash-Shamsu tajriili-musta-qarril-lahaa: zaalika taqdiirul-'Aziizil-'Aliim.

39. Wal-Qamara qaddarnaahu manaazila hattaa 'aada kal-'urjuunil-qadiim.

40. Lash-Shamsu yambagii lahaaa 'an tudrikal-Qamara wa lal-Laylu saabiqun-Nahaar: wa kullun-fii falakiny-yasbahuun.

41. Wa 'Aayatul-lahum 'annaa hamalnaa zurriyyatahum fil-fulki-l-mash-huun;

---

36. Glory to Allah, Who created in pairs all things that the earth produces, as well as their own (human) kind and (other) things of which they have no knowledge.

37. And a Sign for them is the Night: We withdraw therefrom the Day, and behold they are plunged in darkness;

38. And the Sun runs unto a resting place, for him: that is the decree of (Him), the Exalted in Might, the All-Knowing.

39. And the Moon,—We have measured for her stations (to traverse) till she returns like the old (and withered) lower part of a date-stalk.

40. It is not permitted to the Sun to catch up the Moon, nor can the Night outstrip the Day: each (just) swims along in (its own) orbit (according to Law).

41. And a Sign for them is that We bore their race (through the Flood) in the loaded Ark;

42. Wa khalaqnaa lahum-mim-mişlihii maa yarkabuun. وَخَلَقْنَا لَهُمْ مِّنْ مِّثْلِهِ مَا يَرْكَبُونَ ۝

43. Wa 'in-nasha' nugriqhum falaa şariikha lahum wa laa hum yuñqazuun, وَإِنْ نَّشَأْ نُغْرِقْهُمْ فَلَا صَرِيخَ لَهُمْ وَلَا هُمْ يُنْقَذُونَ ۝

44. 'Illaa Rahmatam-minnaa wa mataa-'an 'ilaa hiin. إِلَّا رَحْمَةً مِّنَّا وَمَتَاعًا إِلَى حِينٍ ۝

45. Wa 'izaa qiila lahumuttaquu maa bayna 'aydiikum wa maa khalfakum la-'allakum turhamuun. وَإِذَا قِيلَ لَهُمُ اتَّقُوا مَا بَيْنَ أَيْدِيكُمْ وَمَا خَلْفَكُمْ لَعَلَّكُمْ تُرْحَمُونَ ۝

46. Wa maa ta'-tiihim-min 'Aayatim-min 'Aayaati Rabbihim 'illaa kaanuu 'anhaa mu-'riziin. وَمَا تَأْتِيهِم مِّنْ آيَةٍ مِّنْ آيَاتِ رَبِّهِمْ إِلَّا كَانُوا عَنْهَا مُعْرِضِينَ ۝

47. Wa 'izaa qiila lahum 'añfiquu mim-maa razaqakumul-laahu qaalallaziina kafaruu lillaziina 'aamanuuu 'anut-'imu mallaw yashaaa-'ullaahu 'at-'amah?–'In 'añtum 'illaa fii zalaalim-mubiin. وَإِذَا قِيلَ لَهُمْ أَنْفِقُوا مِمَّا رَزَقَكُمُ اللهُ قَالَ الَّذِينَ كَفَرُوا لِلَّذِينَ آمَنُوا أَنُطْعِمُ مَن لَّوْ يَشَاءُ اللهُ أَطْعَمَهُ إِنْ أَنْتُمْ إِلَّا فِي ضَلَالٍ مُّبِينٍ ۝

48. Wa yaquuluuna mataa haazal-wa-'du 'iñ-kuñtum saadiqiin? وَيَقُولُونَ مَتَى هَذَا الْوَعْدُ إِن كُنتُمْ صَادِقِينَ ۝

---

42. And We have created for them similar (vessels) on which they ride.

43. If it were Our Will, We could drown them: then would there be no helper (to hear their cry), nor could they be delivered,

44. Except by way of Mercy from Us, and by way of (worldly) convenience (to serve them) for a time.

45. When they are told, "Fear ye that which is before you and that which will be after you, in order that ye may receive Mercy," (they turn back).

46. Not a Sign comes to them from among the Signs of their Lord, but they turn away therefrom.

47. And when they are told, "Spend ye of (the bounties) with which Allah has provided you," the Unbelievers say to those who believe: "Shall we then feed those whom, if Allah had so willed, He would have fed, (Himself)?—Ye are in nothing but manifest error."

48. Further, they say, "When will this promise (come to pass), if what ye say is true?"

49. Maa yañ-zuruuna 'illaa Sayha-tañw-waahidatañ ta'-khuzuhum wa hum yakhissimuun! مَايَنْظُرُوْنَ اِلَّا صَيْحَةً وَّاحِدَةً تَأْخُذُهُمْ وَهُمْ يَخِصِّمُوْنَ ۝

50. Falaa yastatii-'uuna tawsi-yatañwwa laaa 'ilaaa 'ahlihim yarji-'uun! (Section 4) فَلَا يَسْتَطِيْعُوْنَ تَوْصِيَةً وَّلَا اِلٰٓى اَهْلِهِمْ يَرْجِعُوْنَ ۝

51. Wa nufikha fiş-Şuuri fa-'izaa hum-minal-'ajdaasi 'ilaa Rabbihim yansiluun ! وَنُفِخَ فِى الصُّوْرِ فَاِذَا هُمْ مِّنَ الْاَجْدَاثِ اِلٰى رَبِّهِمْ يَنْسِلُوْنَ ۝

52. Qaaluu yaa-waylanaa mam-ba-'asanaa mim-marqadinaa-Haazaa maa wa-'adar-Rahmaanu wa sadaqal-mur-saluun ! قَالُوْا يٰوَيْلَنَا مَنْ بَعَثَنَا مِنْ مَّرْقَدِنَا هٰذَا مَا وَعَدَ الرَّحْمٰنُ وَصَدَقَ الْمُرْسَلُوْنَ ۝

53. 'Iñ-kaanat 'illaa Sayha-tañw-waahidatañ fa-'izaa hum jamii-'ul-ladaynaa muhzaruun ! اِنْ كَانَتْ اِلَّا صَيْحَةً وَّاحِدَةً فَاِذَا هُمْ جَمِيْعٌ لَّدَيْنَا مُحْضَرُوْنَ ۝

54. Fal-Yawma laa tuzlamu nafsuñ shay-'añw-wa laa tuj-zawna 'illaa maa kuñtum ta'-maluun. فَالْيَوْمَ لَا تُظْلَمُ نَفْسٌ شَيْئًا وَّلَا تُجْزَوْنَ اِلَّا مَا كُنْتُمْ تَعْمَلُوْنَ ۝

55. 'Inna 'As-haabal-Jannatil-Yawma fii shugulin-faakihuun; اِنَّ اَصْحٰبَ الْجَنَّةِ الْيَوْمَ فِيْ شُغُلٍ فٰكِهُوْنَ ۝

---

49. They will not (have to) wait for aught but a single Blast: it will seize them while they are yet disputing among themselves!

50. No (chance) will they then have, by will, to dispose (of their affairs), nor to return to their own people!

51. The trumpet shall be sounded, when behold! from the sepulchres (men) will rush forth to their Lord!

52. They will say: "Ah! woe unto us! Who hath raised us up from our beds of repose?"...(A voice will say:) "This is what The Most Gracious had promised. And true was the word of the messengers!"

53. It will be no more than a single Blast, when lo! they will all be brought up before Us!

54. Then, on that Day, not a soul will be wronged in the least, and ye shall but be repaid the meeds of your past Deeds.

55. Verily the Companions of the Garden shall that Day have joy in all that they do;

56. Hum wa 'azwaajuhum fii zilaalin 'alal-'araaa-'iki muttaki-'uun;

57. Lahum fiihaa faakihatuṅw-wa lahum-maa yadda-'uun;

58. "Salaam !"–Qawlam-mir Rabbir-Raḥiim !

59. Wamtaazul-Yawma 'ayyuhal-mujrimuun !

60. 'Alam 'a'had 'ilaykum yaa-Baniii-'Aadama 'allaa ta'budush-Shayṭaan; 'innahuu lakum 'aduwwum-mubiin?–

61. Wa 'ani'-buduunii. Haazaa Siraatum-Mustaqiim.

62. Wa laqad 'azalla minkum jibillaṅ-kaṣiiraa. 'Afalam takuunuu ta'qiluun?

63. Haazihii Jahannamullatii kuṅtum tuu-'aduun !

64. 'Islaw-hal-Yawma bimaa kuntum takfuruun.

---

56. They and their associates will be in pleasant shade, reclining on raised couches;

57. (Every) fruit will be there for them; they shall have whatever they call for;

58. "Peace!—a Word (of salutation) from a Lord Most Merciful!

59. "And O ye in sin! Get ye apart this Day!

60. "Did I not enjoin on you, O ye children of Adam, that ye should not worship Satan; for that he was to you an enemy avowed?—

61. "And that ye should worship Me, (for that) this was the Straight Way?

62. "But he did lead astray a great multitude of you. Did ye not, then, understand?

63. "This is the Hell of which ye were promised

64. "Embrace ye the (Fire) this Day, for that ye (persistently) rejected (Truth)."

65. 'Al-Yawma nakhtimu 'alaaa 'af-waahihim wa tukallimunaaa 'aydiihim wa tash-hadu 'arjuluhum-bimaa kaan-uu yaksibuun.

66. Wa law nashaaa-'u latamasnaa 'alaaa 'a'yunihim fastabaqus-Siraata fa-'annaa yubsiruun?

67. Wa law nashaaa-'u lama-sakh-naahum 'alaa makaanati-him famasta-taa-'uu muziyyanwwa laa yarji-'uun. (Section 5)

68. Wa man-nu-'ammirhu nunakkis-hu fil-khalq: 'afalaa ya-'qiluun?

69. Wa maa 'allamnaahush-Shi'ra wa maa yambagii lah: 'in huwa 'illaa Zikrunw-wa Qur-'aanum-Mubiin:

70. Liyunzira man kaana hayyanwwa yahiqqal-qawlu 'alal-kaafiriin.

71. 'Awalam yaraw 'annaa khalaqnaa lahum-mimmaa 'amilat 'aydiinaaa 'an-'aaman fahum lahaa maalikuun?--

---

65. That Day shall We set a seal on their mouths. But their hands will speak to Us, and their feet bear witness, to all that they did.

66. If it had been Our Will, We could surely have blotted out their eyes; then they should have raced to the Path, but how could they have seen?

67. And if it had been Our Will, We could have transformed them in their places; then should they have been unable to move about, nor could they have returned (after error).

68. If We grant long life to any, We cause him to be reversed in nature: will they not then understand?

69. We have not instructed the (Prophet) in Poetry, nor is it meet for him: this is no less than a Message and a Qur'ān making things clear:

70. That it may give admonition to any (who are) alive, and that the word may be proved true against those who reject (Truth).

71. See they not that it is We Who have created for them—among the things which our hands have fashioned— cattle, which are under their dominion?—

72. Wa zallalnaahaa lahum faminhaa rakuubuhum wa minhaa ya'-kuluun:

73. Wa lahum fiihaa manaafi'u wa mashaarib. 'Afalaa yashkuruun?

74. Wattakhazuu min-duunillaahi 'aalihatal-la-'allahum yunsaruun !

75. Laa yastatii-'uuna nasra-hum wa hum lahum jundum-muhzaruun.

76. Falaa yahzunka qawluhum. 'Innaa na'-lamu maa yusirruuna wa maa yu'-linuun.

77. 'Awalam yaral-'insaanu 'annaa khalaqnaahu min-nutfatin fa-'izaa huwa khasiimum-mubiin !

78. Wa zaraba lanaa masalanw wa nasiya khalqah: qaala many-yuhyil-'izaama wa hiya ramiim?

---

72. And that We have subjected them to their (use)? Of them some do carry them and some they eat:

73. And they have (other) profits from them (besides), and they get (milk) to drink. Will they not then be grateful?

74. Yet they take (for worship) Gods other than Allah, (hoping) that they might be helped!

75. They have not the power to help them: and they are a host brought up before them.

76. Let not their speech, then, grieve thee. Verily We know what they hide as well as what they disclose.

77. Doth not man see that it is We Who created him from sperm? Yet behold! he (stands forth) as an open adversary!

78. And he makes comparisons for Us, and forgets his own (origin and) Creation: He says, "Who can give life to (dry) bones and decomposed ones (at that)?"

79. Qul yuḥyiihallaziii ’ansha-
’ahaaa ’awwala marrah! Wa Huwa
bi-kulli khalqin ‘Aliim !

قُلْ يُحْيِيهَا الَّذِىٓ أَنشَأَهَآ أَوَّلَ مَرَّةٍ ۖ وَهُوَ بِكُلِّ خَلْقٍ عَلِيمٌ ۝

80. ’Allazii ja-‘ala lakum-minash-
shajaril-’akhẓari naarañ fa-’izaaa ’añ-
tum-minhu tuuqiduun!

الَّذِى جَعَلَ لَكُم مِّنَ الشَّجَرِ الْأَخْضَرِ نَارًا فَإِذَآ أَنتُم مِّنْهُ تُوقِدُونَ ۝

81. ’Awa laysallazii khalaqas-
samaawaati wal-’arẓa bi-Qaadirin
‘alaaa ’añyyakhluqa miṣlahum?--
Balaa! wa Huwal-Khallaaqul-‘Aliim!

أَوَلَيْسَ الَّذِى خَلَقَ السَّمَٰوَٰتِ وَالْأَرْضَ بِقَٰدِرٍ عَلَىٰٓ أَن يَخْلُقَ مِثْلَهُم ۚ بَلَىٰ وَهُوَ الْخَلَّٰقُ الْعَلِيمُ ۝

82. ’Innamaaa ’Amruhuuu ’izaaa
’araada shay-’añ ’anyyaquula lahuu
“KUÑ” fayakuun !

إِنَّمَآ أَمْرُهُۥٓ إِذَآ أَرَادَ شَيْئًا أَن يَقُولَ لَهُۥ كُن فَيَكُونُ ۝

83. Fa-Subḥaanallazii bi-yadihii
Malakuutu kulli shay-’iñwwa ’ilayhi
turja-‘uun.

فَسُبْحَٰنَ الَّذِى بِيَدِهِۦ مَلَكُوتُ كُلِّ شَىْءٍ وَإِلَيْهِ تُرْجَعُونَ ۝

---

79. Say, “He will give them life Who created them for the first time!
For He fully knows all creation.

80. “The same Who produces for you fire out of the green tree, when
behold! Ye kindle therewith (your own fires)!

81. “Is not He Who created the heavens and the earth able to create
the like thereof?”-- Yea, indeed! For He is the Creator Supreme,
of skill and knowledge (infinite)!

82. Verily, when He intends a thing, His Command is, “Be”, and it is!

83. So glory to Him in Whose Hands is the dominion of all things:
and to Him will ye be all brought back.

Fath–48
Verses 29–Sections 4

Bismillaahir-Rahmaanir-Rahiim.

1.　'Innaa fatahnaa laka Fatham-Mubiinaa,

2.　Liyagfira lakallaahu maa taqaddama min-zambika wa maa ta-'akh-khara wa yutimma ni'-matahuu 'alayka wa yahdi-yaka Siraatam-Mustaqiimaa,

3.　Wa yansurakallaahu Nasran 'Aziizaa.

4.　Huwallazii 'anzalas-Sakiinata fii quluubil-Mu'-miniina liyazdaaduuu 'iimaanam-ma-'a 'iimaanihim; wa lillaahi Junuu-dus-samaawaati wal-'arz; wa kaanallaahu 'Aliiman Hakiimaa,

Al-Fath or Victory

In the name of Allah, Most Gracious Most Merciful.

1.　Verily We have granted thee a manifest Victory:

2.　That Allah may forgive thee thy faults of the past and those to follow; fulfil His favour to thee; and guide thee on the Straight Way;

3.　And that Allah may help thee with powerful help.

4.　It is He Who sent down Tranquillity into the hearts of the Believers, that they may add Faith to their Faith;— for to Allah belong the Forces of the heavens and the earth; and Allah is Full of Knowledge and Wisdom;—

5. Li-yud-khilal-Mu'-miniina wal-Mu'-minaati Jannaatiñ-taj-rii miñ-tahtihal-'anhaaru khaalidiina fiihaa wa yukaffira 'an-hum sayyi-'aatihim; —wa kaa-na zaalika 'indallaahi fawzan 'aziimaa,--

لِيُدْخِلَ الْمُؤْمِنِيْنَ وَالْمُؤْمِنٰتِ جَنّٰتٍ تَجْرِىْ مِنْ تَحْتِهَا الْاَنْهٰرُ خٰلِدِيْنَ فِيْهَا وَيُكَفِّرَ عَنْهُمْ سَيِّاٰتِهِمْ ۚ وَكَانَ ذٰلِكَ عِنْدَ اللّٰهِ فَوْزًا عَظِيْمًا ۙ ٥

6. Wa yu-'azzibal-Munaafiqiina wal-Munaafiqaati wal-Mushri-kiina wal-Mushrikaatiz-zaaan-niina billaahi zannas-saw'. 'Alay-him daaa-'iratus-saw': wa gaziballaahu 'alay-him wa la-'anahum wa 'a-'adda lahum Jahannam: wa saaa-'at masii-raa.

وَيُعَذِّبَ الْمُنٰفِقِيْنَ وَالْمُنٰفِقٰتِ وَ الْمُشْرِكِيْنَ وَالْمُشْرِكٰتِ الظَّآنِّيْنَ بِاللّٰهِ ظَنَّ السَّوْءِ ؕ عَلَيْهِمْ دَآئِرَةُ السَّوْءِ ۚ وَ غَضِبَ اللّٰهُ عَلَيْهِمْ وَلَعَنَهُمْ وَاَعَدَّ لَهُمْ جَهَنَّمَ ؕ وَسَآءَتْ مَصِيْرًا ٦

7. Wa lillaahi Junuudus-samaa-waati wal-'arz: wa kaanallaahu 'Aziizan Hakiimaa.

وَلِلّٰهِ جُنُوْدُ السَّمٰوٰتِ وَالْاَرْضِ ؕ وَكَانَ اللّٰهُ عَزِيْزًا حَكِيْمًا ٧

8. 'Innaaa 'arsalnaaka Shaahidanw-wa Mubash-shiranw-wa Naziiraa:

اِنَّاۤ اَرْسَلْنٰكَ شَاهِدًا وَّمُبَشِّرًا وَّ نَذِيْرًا ۙ ٨

---

5. That He may admit the men and women who believe, to Gardens beneath which rivers flow, to dwell therein for aye, and remove their sins from them;—and that is, in the sight of Allah, the grand triumph,

6. And that He may punish the Hypocrites, men and women, and the Polytheists, men and women, who think an evil thought of Allah. On them is a round of Evil: the Wrath of Allah is on them: He has cursed them and got Hell ready for them: and evil is it for a destination.

7. For to Allah belong the Forces of the heavens and the earth; and Allah is exalted in Power, Full of Wisdom.

8. We have truly sent thee as a witness, as a bringer of Glad Tidings, and as a Warner:

9. Litu'-minuu billaahi wa Rasuulihii wa tu-'azziruuhu wa tuwaqqiruuh, wa tusabbihuuhu bukratanw-wa 'asiilaa.

10. 'Innallaziina yubaa-yi-'uu-naka 'innamaa yubaayi-'uunal-laah: Yadullaahi fawqa 'aydii-him: faman-nakasa fa-'inna-maa yankusu 'alaa nafsih; wa man 'awfaa bimaa 'aahada 'alay-hullaaha fasayu'-tiihi 'aj-ran 'aziimaa. (Section 2)

11. Sayaquulu lakal-mukhalla-fuuna minal-'A'-raabi shagalat-naaa 'amwaalunaa wa 'ahluu-naa fastagfir lanaa. Yaquuluu-na bi-'alsinatihim-maa laysa fii quluubihim. Qul famany-yam-liku lakum-minallaahi shay-'an 'in 'araada bikum zarran 'aw 'araada bikum naf-'aa? Bal kaanallaahu bimaa ta'-maluu-na khabiiraa.

---

9. In order that ye (O men) may believe in Allah and His Messenger, that ye may assist and honour him, and celebrate His praises morning and evening.

10. Verily those who plight their fealty to thee plight their fealty in truth to Allah: the Hand of Allah is over their hands: then anyone who violates his oath, does so to the harm of his own soul, and anyone who fulfils what he has covenanted with Allah,— Allah will soon grant him a great Reward.

11. The desert Arabs who lagged behind will say to thee: "We were engaged in (looking after) our flocks and herds, and our families: do thou then ask forgiveness for us." They say with their tongues what is not in their hearts. Say: "Who then has any power at all (to intervene) on your behalf with Allah, if His Will is to give you some loss or to give you some profit? But Allah is well acquainted with all that ye do.

12. Bal ẓanantum 'allany-yan-qalibar-Rasuulu wal-Mu'-minuuna 'ilaaa 'ahliihim 'abadanwwa zuyyina zaalika fii quluubikum wa zanantum zannas-saw-'i wa kuntum qaw-mam-buuraa.

13. Wa mal-lam yu'-mim-billaahi wa Rasuulihii fa-'innaaa 'a'-tadnaa lil-kaafiriina Sa-'ii-raa!

14. Wa lillaahi Mulkus-samaawaati wal-'arẓ: yagfiru limany-yashaaa-'u wa yu-'azzibu many-yashaaa': wa kaanal-laahu Gafuurar-Raḥiimaa.

15. Sayaquulul-mukhallafuuna 'izan-talaqtum 'ilaa magaanima lita'-khuẓuuhaa zaruunaa nattabi'-kum: yurii-duuna 'any-yubaddiluu Kalaa-mallaah. Qul-lan-tattabi-'uunaa ka-zaalikum qaalallaahu min-qabl: fasayaquuluuna bal taḥsuduunanaa. Bal kaanuu laa yaf-qahuuna 'illaa qaliilaa.

---

12. 'Nay ye thought that the Messenger and the Believers would never return to their families; this seemed pleasing in your hearts, and ye conceived an evil thought, for ye are a people doomed to perish."

13. And if any believe not in Allah and His Messenger, We have prepared, for those who reject Allah, a Blazing Fire!

14. To Allah belongs the dominion of the heavens and the earth: He forgives whom He wills, and He punishes whom He wills: but Allah is Oft-Forgiving, Most Merciful.

15. Those who lagged behind (will say), when ye set forth to acquire booty (in war): "Permit us to follow you." They wish to change Allah's word: say: "Not thus will ye follow us: Allah has already declared (this) beforehand": then they will say, "But ye are jealous of us." Nay, but little do they understand (such things).

16. Qul-lil-mukhallafiina minal-'A'-raabi satud-'awna 'ilaa qawmin 'ulii ba'-siñ-shadiidin-tuqaatiluunahum 'aw yuslimuun. Fa-'iñ-tutii-'uu yu'ti-kumullaahu 'ajran hasanaa; wa 'iñ-tatawallaw kamaa tawallay-tum-miñ-qablu yu-'azzibkum 'azaaban 'aliimaa.

17. Laysa 'alal-'a'-maa hara-juñw-wa laa 'alal-'a'-raji hara- juñw-wa laa 'alal-mariizi haraj. Wa many-yuti-'illaaha wa Rasuulahuu yudkhilhu Jannaa-tiñ-tajrii miñ-tahtihal-'anhaar; wa many-yatawalla yu-'azzibhu 'azaaban 'aliimaa. (Part One-half) (Section 3)

18. Laqad razi-yallaahu 'anil-Mu'-miniina 'iz yubaa-yi-'uu-naka tahtash-Shajarati fa-'alima maa fii-quluubihim fa-'añzalas-Sakiinata 'alayhim wa 'asaabahum Fat-hañ-qariibaa;

---

16. Say to the desert Arabs who lagged behind: "Ye shall be summoned (to fight) against a people given to vehement war: then shall ye fight, or they shall submit. Then if ye show obedience, Allah will grant you a goodly reward, but if ye turn back as ye did before, He will punish you with a grievous Chastisement."

17. No blame is there on the blind, nor is there blame on the lame, nor on one ill (if he joins not the war): but he that obeys Allah and His Messenger,—(Allah) will admit him to Gardens beneath which rivers flow; and he who turns back, (Allah) will punish him with a grievous Chastisement.

18. Allah's Good Pleasure was on the Believers when they swore Fealty to thee under the Tree: He knew what was in their hearts, and He sent down Tranquillity to them; and He rewarded them with a speedy Victory;

19. Wa magaanima kasiiratany-ya'-khuzuunahaa: wa kaanallaahu 'Aziizan Hakiimaa.

20. Wa-'adakumullaahu magaanima kasiiratan ta'-khuzuu-nahaa fa-'ajjala lakum haazihii wa kaffa 'aydiyannaasi 'an-kum; wa litakuuna 'Aayatal-lil-Mu'miniina wa yahdiyakum Siraatam-Mustaqiimaa;

21. Wa 'ukhraa lam taqdiruu 'alayhaa qad 'ahaatallaahu bi-haa: wa kaanallaahu 'alaa kulli shay-'in-Qadiiraa.

22. Wa law qaatalakumullaziina kafaruu lawalla-wul-'adbaara summa laa yajiduuna waliyyanw-wa laa nasiiraa.

23. Sunnatallaahillatii qad khalat min-qablu wa lan-tajida li-Sunnatillaahi tabdiilaa.

---

19. And many gains will they acquire (besides): and Allah is Exalted in Power, Full of Wisdom.

20. Allah has promised you many gains that ye shall acquire, and He has given you these beforehand; and He has restrained the hands of men from you; that it may be a Sign for the Believers, and that He may guide you to a Straight Path;

21. And other gains (there are), which are not within your power, but which Allah has compassed: and Allah has power over all things.

22. If the Unbelievers should fight you, they would certainly turn their backs; then would they find neither protector nor helper.

23. (Such has been) the practice of Allah already in the past: no change wilt thou find in the practice of Allah.

24. Wa Huwallazii kaffa 'aydi-yahum 'ankum wa 'aydiyakum 'anhum bi-batni Makkata mim-ba'-di 'an 'azfarakum 'alay-him. Wa kaanallaahu bimaa ta'-maluuna Basiiraa.

وَهُوَالَّذِيْ كَفَّ أَيْدِيَهُمْ عَنْكُمْ وَأَيْدِيَكُمْ عَنْهُمْ بِبَطْنِ مَكَّةَ مِنْ بَعْدِ أَنْ أَظْفَرَكُمْ عَلَيْهِمْ ۚ وَكَانَ اللّٰهُ بِمَا تَعْمَلُوْنَ بَصِيْرًا ۝

25. Humullaziina kafaruu wa sadduukum 'anil-Masjidil-Ha-raami wal-hadya ma'-kuufan 'any-yablugha mahillah. Wa law laa rijaalum-Mu'-minuuna wa nisaaa-'um-Mu'-minaatul-lam ta'-lamuuhum 'an-tata-'uuhum fatusiibakum-minhum-ma-'arratum-bi-gayri 'ilm, li-yudkhilallaahu fii Rahmatihii many-yashaaa'. Law tazayyaluu la-'azzabnallaziina kafaruu minhum 'azaaban 'aliimaa.

هُمُ الَّذِيْنَ كَفَرُوْا وَصَدُّوْكُمْ عَنِ الْمَسْجِدِ الْحَرَامِ وَالْهَدْىَ مَعْكُوْفًا أَنْ يَّبْلُغَ مَحِلَّهٗ ۚ وَلَوْلَا رِجَالٌ مُّؤْمِنُوْنَ وَنِسَاءٌ مُّؤْمِنَاتٌ لَّمْ تَعْلَمُوْهُمْ أَنْ تَطَئُوْهُمْ فَتُصِيْبَكُمْ مِّنْهُمْ مَّعَرَّةٌ بِغَيْرِ عِلْمٍ ۚ لِيُدْخِلَ اللّٰهُ فِيْ رَحْمَتِهٖ مَنْ يَّشَاءُ ۚ لَوْ تَزَيَّلُوْا لَعَذَّبْنَا الَّذِيْنَ كَفَرُوْا مِنْهُمْ عَذَابًا أَلِيْمًا ۝

---

24. And it is He Who has restrained their hands from you and your hands from them in the valley of Makkah, after that He gave you the victory over them. And Allah sees well all that ye do.

25. They are the ones who disbelieved and hindered you from the Sacred Mosque and the sacrificial animals, detained from reaching their place of sacrifice. Had there not been believing men and believing women whom ye did not know that ye were trampling down and on whose account a guilt would have accrued to you without (your) knowledge, (Allah would have allowed you to force your way, but He held back your hands) that He may admit to His Mercy whom He will. If they had been apart, We should certainly have punished the Unbelievers among them with a grievous Punishment.

26. 'Iz ja-'alallaziina kafaruu fii quluubihimul-hamiyyata Hamiyyatal-Jaahi-liyyati fa-'anzalallaahu Sakiinatahuu 'alaa Rasuulihii wa 'alal-Mu'-miniina wa 'alzamahum kali-matat-taqwaa wa kaanuuu 'ahaqqa bihaa wa 'ahlahaa. Wa kaanallaahu bi-kulli shay-'in 'Aliimaa. (Section 4)

27. Laqad sadaqallaahu Rasuulahur-ru'-yaa bil-haqq: latad-khulunnal-Masjidal-Haraama 'in-shaaa-'allaahu 'aaminiina muhalliqiina ru-'uusakum wa muqassiriina laatakhaafuun. Fa-'alima maa lam ta'-lamuu faja-'ala min-duuni zaalika fat-han-qariibaa.

28. Huwallaziii 'arsala Rasuu-lahuu bil-Hudaa wa Diinil-Haqqi liyuzhirahuu 'alad-diini kullih: wa kafaa billaahi Shahiidaa.

---

26.   While the Unbelievers got up in their hearts heat and cant—the heat and cant of Ignorance,— Allah sent down His Tranquillity to His Messenger and to the Believers, and made them stick close to the command of self-restraint; and well were they entitled to it and worthy of it. And Allah has full knowledge of all things.

27.   Truly did Allah fulfil the vision for His Messenger: ye shall enter the Sacred Mosque, if Allah wills, with minds secure, heads shaved, hair cut short, and without fear. For He knew what ye knew not, and He granted, besides this, a speedy victory.

28.   It is He Who has sent His Messenger with Guidance and the Religion of Truth, to make it prevail over all religion: and enough is Allah for a Witness.

29. Muhammadur-Rasuulul-laah: wallaziina ma-'ahuuu 'a-shid-daaa-'u 'alal-kuffaari ruha-maaa-'u baynahum taraahum rukka-'añ-sujjadañy-yabtaguu-na Fazlam-minallaahi wa Rizwaanaa. Siimaahum fii wujuuhihim-min 'asaris-sujuud. Zaalika masaluhum fit-Tawraati wa masaluhum fil-'Iñjiil: kazar-'in 'akhraja shat-'ahuu fa-'aazarahuu fastaglaza fastawaa 'alaa suuqihii yu'-jibuz-zurraa-'a li-yagiiza bihimul-kuffaar. Wa-'adallaa-hullaziina 'aamanuu wa 'amilus-saalihaati minhum-Magfirataňw-wa 'Ajran 'aziimaa.

---

29.   Muhammad is the Messenger of Allah; and those who are with him are strong against Unbelievers, (but) compassionate amongst each other. Thou wilt see them bow and prostrate themselves (in prayer), seeking Grace from Allah and (His) Good Pleasure. On their faces are their marks, (being) the traces of their prostration. This is their similitude in the Taurāt; and their similitude in the Gospel is: Like a seed which sends forth its blade, then makes it strong; it then becomes thick, and it stands on its own stem, (filling) the sowers with wonder and delight. As a result, it fills the Unbelievers with rage at them. Allah has promised those among them who believe and do righteous deeds forgiveness, and a great Reward.

Rahmaan–55
Verses 78–Sections 3

Bismillaahir-Raḥmaanir-Raḥiim.

1. 'AR -RAHMAANU
2. 'Allamal-Qur-'aan.
3. Khalaqal-'insaana
4. 'Allamahul-bayaan.
5. 'Ash-shamsu wal-qamaru bihusbaan;
6. Wan-najmu wash-shajaru yasjudaan.
7. Was-Samaaa-'a rafa-'ahaa wa waza-'al-Miizaana
8. 'Allaa taṭ-gaw fil-miizaan.

9. Wa'aqiimul-waznabil-qisṭi wa laa tukh-sirul-miizaan.
10. Wal-'arza waza-'ahaa lil-'anaam:
11. Fiihaa faakihatuñw-wan-nakhlu zaatul-'akmaam;
12. Wal-habbu zul-'asfi war-rayhaan.

Ar-Rahmãn, or (Allah) Most Gracious

In the name of Allah, Most Gracious, Most Merciful.

1. The Most Gracious!
2. It is He Who has taught the Qur'ãn
3. He has created man:
4. He has taught him an intelligent speech.
5. The sun and the moon follow courses (exactly) computed;
6. And the herbs and the trees— both (alike) bow in adoration.
7. And the Firmament has He raised high, and He has set up the Balance (of Justice),
8. In order that ye may not transgress (due) balance.
9. So establish weight with justice and fall not short in the balance.
10. It is He Who has spread out the earth for (His) creatures:
11. Therein is fruit and date-palms, producing spathes (enclosing dates);
12. Also corn, with (its) leaves and stalk for fodder, and sweet-smelling plants.

13. Fabi-'ayyi 'aalaaa-'i Rabbikumaa tukazzibaan?

14. Khalaqal-'insaana min salsaalin-kal-fakh-khaar,

15. Wa khalaqal-Jaaanna 'mim-maarijim-min-Naar:

16. Fabi-'ayyi 'aalaaa-'i Rabbikumaa tukazzibaan?

17. Rabbul-Mashri-qayni wa Rabbul-Magribayn:

18. Fabi-'ayyi 'aalaaa-'i Rabbikumaa tukazzibaan?

19. Marajal-bah-rayni yal-taqiyaan:

20. Baynahumaa Barzakhullaa yabgi-yaan:

21. Fabi-'ayyi 'aalaaa-'i Rabbikumaa tukazzibaan?

22. Yakhruju minhumal-Lu'-lu-'u wal-Marjaan:

23. Fabi-'ayyi 'aalaaa-'i Rabbikumaa tukazzibaan?

24. Wa lahul-Jawaaril-munsha-'aatu fil-bahri kal-'a'-laam:

25. Fabi-'ayyi 'aalaaa-'i Rabbikumaa tukazzibaan? (Section 2) (Part One Half)

---

13. Then which of the favours of your Lord will ye deny?

14. He created man from sounding clay like unto pottery,

15. And He created Jinns from fire free of smoke:

16. Then which of the favours of your Lord will ye deny?

17. (He is) Lord of the two Easts and Lord of the two Wests:

18. Then which of the favours of your Lord will ye deny?

19. He has let free the two Seas meeting together:

20. Between them is a Barrier which they do not transgress:

21. Then which of the favours of your Lord will ye deny?

22. Out of them come Pearls and Coral:

23. Then which of the favours of your Lord will ye deny?

24. And His are the Ships sailing smoothly through the seas, lofty as mountains:

25. Then which of the favours of your Lord will ye deny?

26. Kullu man 'alay-haa faan:

27. Wa yabqaa Wajhu Rabbika Zul-Jalaali wal-'Ikraam.

28. Fabi-'ayyi 'aalaaa-'i Rabbikumaa tukazzibaan?

29. Yas-'aluhuu man-fis-samaa-waati wal-arz: kulla Yawmin Huwa fii sha'-n!

30. Fabi-'ayyi 'aalaaa-'i Rabbikumaa tukazzibaan?

31. Sanafrugu lakum 'ayyuhas-saqalaan!

32. Fabi-'ayyi 'aalaaa-'i Rabbikumaa tukazzibaan?

33. Yaa-Ma'-sharal-jinni wal-'insi 'inistata'-tum 'an tanfuzuu min 'aqtaaris-samaawaati wal-'arzi fanfuzuu! laa tanfuzuuna 'illaa bisul-taan!

34. Fabi-'ayyi 'aalaaa-'i Rabbikumaa tukazzibaan?

35. Yursalu 'alaykumaa shu-waazum-min-naarinw-wa nu-haasun-falaa tantasiraan:

---

26. All that is on earth will perish:

27. But will abide (for ever) the Face of thy Lord,— full of Majesty, Bounty and Honour.

28. Then which of the favours of your Lord will ye deny?

29. Of Him seeks (its need) every creature in the heavens and on earth: every day in (new) Splendour doth He (shine)!

30. Then which of the favours of your Lord will ye deny?

31. Soon shall We settle your affairs, O both ye worlds!

32. Then which of the favours of your Lord will ye deny?

33. O ye assembly of Jinns and men! If it be ye can pass beyond the zones of the heavens and the earth, pass ye! Not without authority shall ye be able to pass!

34. Then which of the favours of your Lord will ye deny?

35. On you will be sent (O ye evil ones twain!) a flame of fire (to burn) and a (flash of) molten brass no defence will ye have:

36. Fabi-'ayyi 'aalaaa-'i Rabbikumaa tukazzibaan?

37. Fa-'izan-shaqqatis-samaaa-'u fakaanat wardatan-kad-dihaan:

38. Fabi-'ayyi 'aalaaa-'i Rabbikumaa tukazzibaan?

39. Fayawma -'izil-laa yus-'alu 'an-zambihiii 'insunw-wa laa jaaann,–

40. Fabi-'ayyi 'aalaaa-'i Rabbikumaa tukazzibaan?

41. Yu'-raful-mujrimuuna bi-siimaahum fa-yu'-khazu bin-nawaasii wal-'aqdaam:

42. Fabi-'ayyi 'aalaaa-'i Rabbikumaa tukazzibaan?

43. Haazihii Jahannamullatii yukazzibu bihal-mujrimuun:

44. Yatuufuuna baynahaa wa bayna hamiimin 'aan!

45. Fabi-'ayyi 'aalaaa-'i Rabbikumaa tukazzibaan? (Section 3)

---

36. Then which of the favours of your Lord will ye deny?

37. When the sky is rent asunder, and it becomes red like ointment:

38. Then which of the favours of your Lord will ye deny?

39. On that Day no question will be asked of man or Jinn as to his sin,

40. Then which of the favours of your Lord will ye deny?

41. (For) the sinners will be known by their Marks: and they will be seized by their forelocks and their feet.

42. Then which of the favours of your Lord will ye deny?

43. This is the Hell which the Sinners deny:

44. In its midst and in the midst of boiling hot water will they wander round!

45. Then which of the favours of your Lord will ye deny?

46. Wa liman khaafa maqaama Rabbihii Jannataan,–
47. Fabi-'ayyi 'aalaaa-'i Rabbikumaa tukazzibaan?

48. Zawaataaa 'afnaan;–
49. Fabi-'ayyi 'aalaaa-'i Rabbikumaa tukazzibaan?

50. Fiihimaa 'aynaani tajriyaan:–

51. Fabi-'ayyi 'aalaaa-'i Rabbikumaa tukazzibaan?
52. Fiihimaa min-kulli faakihatin-zawjaan.
53. Fabi-'ayyi 'aalaaa-'i Rabbikumaa tukazzibaan?
54. Muttaki-'iina 'alaa furushim-bataaa-'inuhaa min 'istabraq: wa ja-nal-jannatayni daan.
55. Fabi-'ayyi 'aalaaa-'i Rabbikumaa tukazzibaan?
56. Fiihinna qaasiraatut-tarfilam yatmis-hunna 'insun-qabla-hum wa laa jaaann;–

---

46. But for such as fear the time when they will stand before (the Judgment Seat of) their Lord, there will be two Gardens—
47. Then which of the favours of your Lord will ye deny?—
48. Abounding in branches,—
49. Then which of the favours of your Lord will ye deny?—
50. In them (each) will be two Springs flowing (free);
51. Then which of the favours of your Lord will ye deny?—
52. In them will be Fruits of every kind, two and two.
53. Then which of the favours of your Lord will ye deny?
54. They will recline on Carpets, whose inner linings will be of rich brocade: the Fruit of the Gardens will be near (and easy of reach).
55. Then which of the favours of your Lord will ye deny?
56. In them will be (Maidens), chaste, restraining their glances, whom no man or Jinn before them has touched;—

57. Fabi-'ayyi 'aalaaa-'i Rabbikumaa tukazzibaan?

58. Ka-'anna-hunnal-yaaquutu wal-marjaan.

59. Fabi-'ayyi 'aalaaa-'i Rabbikumaa tukazzibaan?

60. Hal-Jazaaa-ul-'Iḥsaani 'illal-'Iḥsaan?

61. Fabi-'ayyi 'aalaaa-'i Rabbikumaa tukazzibaan?

62. Wa min-duunihimaa Jannataan,–

63. Fabi-'ayyi 'aalaaa-'i Rabbikumaa tukazzibaan?

64. Mud-haaam-mataan.

65. Fabi-'ayyi 'aalaaa-'i Rabbikumaa tukazzibaan?

66. Fiihimaa 'aynaani nazzaa-khataan:

67. Fabi-'ayyi 'aalaaa-'i Rabbikumaa tukazzibaan?

68. Fiihimaa faakihatunw-wa nakhlunw-wa rummaan:

69. Fabi-'ayyi 'aalaaa-'i Rabbikumaa tukazzibaan?

---

57. Then which of the favours of your Lord will ye deny?

58. Like unto rubies and coral.

59. Then which of the favours of your Lord will ye deny?

60. Is there any Reward for Good-other than Good?

61. Then which of the favours of your Lord will ye deny?

62. And besides these two, there are two other Gardens,—

63. Then which of the favours of your Lord will ye deny?—

64. Dark-green in colour (from plentiful watering).

65. Then which of the favours of your Lord will ye deny?

66. In them (each) will be two Springs pouring forth water in continuous abundance:

67. Then which of the favours of your Lord will ye deny?

68. In them will be Fruits, and dates and pomegranates:

69. Then which of the favours of your Lord will ye deny?

70. Fiihinna khay-raatun hisaan;–

71. Fabi-'ayyi 'aalaaa-'i Rabbikumaa tukazzibaan?

72. Huurum-maq-suuraatun-fil-khiyaam;–

73. Fabi-'ayyi 'aalaaa-'i Rabbikumaa tukazzibaan?

74. Lam yatmis-hunna 'insun-qablahum wa laa jaaann;

75. Fabi-'ayyi 'aalaaa-'i Rabbikumaa tukazzibaan?

76. Muttaki-'iina 'alaa raf-rafin khuzrinw-wa 'ab-qariy-yin hisaan.

77. Fabi-'ayyi 'aalaaa-'i Rabbikumaa tukazzibaan?

78. Tabaarakas-mu Rabbika Zil-Jalaali wal-'Ikraam.

---

70. In them will be fair (Maidens), good, beautiful;—

71. Then which of the favours of your Lord will ye deny?—

72. Maidens restrained (as to their glances), in (goodly) pavilions:—

73. Then which of the favours of your Lord will ye deny?—

74. Whom no man or Jinn before them has touched;—

75. Then which of the favours of your Lord will ye deny?—

76. Reclining on green Cushions and rich Carpets of beauty.

77. Then which of the favours of your Lord will ye deny?

78. Blessed be the name of thy Lord, Full of Majesty, Bounty and Honour.

Waaqi-'ah–56
Verses 96–Sections 3

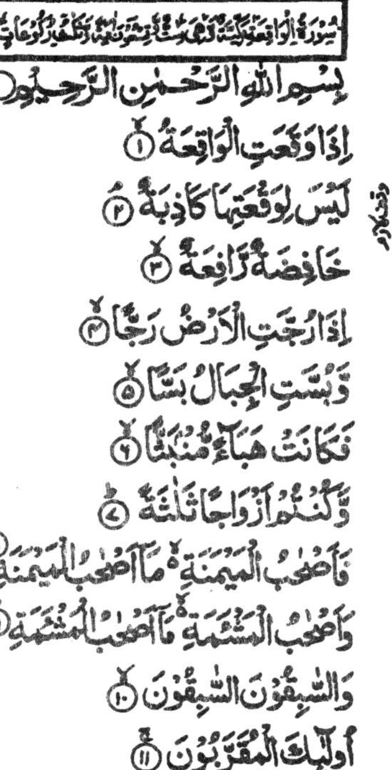

Bismillaahir-Rahmaanir-Rahiim.

1. 'Izaa waqa-'atil-WAAQI-'AH,

2. Laysa li-waq-'atihaa kaazibah.

3. Khaafizatur-Raafi-'ah;

4. 'Izaa rujjatil-'arzu rajjaa,

5. Wa bussatil-jibaalu bassaa,

6. Fakaanat habaaa-'am-mum-bassaa,

7. Wakuntum 'azwaajan-salaasah.

8. Fa-'As-haabul-May-manah; Maaa 'As-haabul-May-manah?

9. Wa 'As-haabul-mash-'amah,– Maaa 'As-haabul-Mash-'amah?

10. Was-Saabiquunas-Saabiquun.

11. 'Ulaaa-'ikal-Muqarrabuun:

Al-Wāqi'a, or The Inevitable Event

In the name of Allah, Most Gracious, Most Merciful.

1. When the Event Inevitable cometh to pass,
2. Then will no (soul) deny its coming.
3. (Many) will it bring low; (many) will it exalt;
4. When the earth shall be shaken to its depths,
5. And the mountains shall be crumbled to atoms,
6. Becoming dust scattered abroad,
7. And ye shall be sorted out into three classes.
8. Then (there will be) the Companions of the Right Hand;— what will be the Companions of the Right Hand?
9. And the Companions of the Left Hand,— what will be the Companions of the Left Hand!
10. And those Foremost (in Faith) will be foremost (in the Hereafter).
11. These will be those Nearest to Allah:

12. Fii Jannaatin-Na-'iim:

فِىۡ جَنّٰتِ النَّعِيۡمِ ۝

13. Sullatum-minal-'awwaliin,

ثُلَّةٌ مِّنَ الۡاَوَّلِيۡنَ ۝

14. Wa qaliilum-minal-'aa-khiriin.

وَقَلِيۡلٌ مِّنَ الۡاٰخِرِيۡنَ ۝

15. 'Alaa sururim-maw-zuunah,

عَلٰى سُرُرٍ مَّوۡضُوۡنَةٍ ۝

16. Muttaki-'iina 'alay-haa mutaqaabiliin.

مُّتَّكِئِيۡنَ عَلَيۡهَا مُتَقٰبِلِيۡنَ ۝

17. Yatuufu 'alay-him wildaanum-mukhalla-duun

يَطُوۡفُ عَلَيۡهِمۡ وِلۡدَانٌ مُّخَلَّدُوۡنَ ۝

18. Bi-'akwaabinw-wa 'abaa-riiqa, wa ka'-sim-mim-ma-'iin:

بِاَكۡوَابٍ وَّاَبَارِيۡقَ ۙ وَكَاۡسٍ مِّنۡ مَّعِيۡنٍ ۝

19. Laa yusadda-'uuna 'anhaa wa laa yunzifuun:

لَّا يُصَدَّعُوۡنَ عَنۡهَا وَلَا يُنۡزِفُوۡنَ ۝

20. Wa faaki-hatim-mimmaa yata-khayya-ruun;

وَفَاكِهَةٍ مِّمَّا يَتَخَيَّرُوۡنَ ۝

21. Wa lahmi tayrim-mimmaa yashta-huun.

وَلَحۡمِ طَيۡرٍ مِّمَّا يَشۡتَهُوۡنَ ۝

22. Wa huurun 'iin,–

وَحُوۡرٌ عِيۡنٌ ۝

23. Ka-'amsaalil-lu'-lu-'il-maknuun.

كَاَمۡثَالِ اللُّؤۡلُؤِ الۡمَكۡنُوۡنِ ۝

---

12. In Gardens of Bliss:
13. A number of people from those of old,
14. And a few from those of later times.
15. (They will be) on couches encrusted (with gold and precious stones),
16. Reclining on them, facing each other.
17. Round about them will (serve) youths of perpetual (freshness),
18. With goblets, (shining) beakers, and cups (filled) out of clear-flowing fountains:
19. No after-ache will they receive therefrom, nor will they suffer intoxication:
20. And with fruits, any that they may select;
21. And the flesh of fowls, any that they may desire.
22. And (there will be) Companions with beautiful, big, and lustrous eyes,—
23. Like unto Pearls well-guarded.

24. Jazaaa-'am-bimaa kaanuu ya'-maluun.

25. Laa yasma-'uuna fiihaa lag-wanw-wa laa ta'-siimaa,–

26. 'Illaa qiilan-Salaaman-Salaamaa.

27. Wa'As-haabul-Yamiin,–maaa 'As-haabul-yamiin?

28. Fii sidrim-makhzuud,–

29. Wa talhim-manzuud,–

30. Wa zillim-mamduud,

31. Wa maaa-'im-maskuub,

32. Wa faakihatin-kasiirah,

33. Laa maq-tuu-'a-tinw-wa laa mamnuu-'ah,

34. Wa furushim-marfuu-'ah.

35. 'Innaaa 'ansha'-naahunna 'inshaaa-'aa,

36. Faja-'alnaa-hunna 'abkaa-raa,–

37. 'Uruban 'atraabaa,

---

24. A Reward for the Deeds of their past (Life).
25. No frivolity will they hear therein, nor any Mischief,—
26. Only the Saying, "Peace! Peace"
27. The Companions of the Right Hand,— what will be the Companions of the Right Hand!
28. (They will be) among Lote-trees without thorns,
29. Among Talh trees with flowers (or fruits) piled one above another,—
30. In shade long-extended,
31. By water flowing constantly,
32. And fruit in abundance.
33. Whose season is not limited, nor (supply) forbidden,
34. And on couches raised high.
35. We have created them of special creation.
36. And made them virgin-pure (and undefiled),—
37. Full of love (for their mates) equal in age,—

38. Li-'As-haabil-Yamiin. (Section 2)

39. Sullatum-minal-'awwaliin.

40. Wa sullatum-minal-'aakhiriin.

41. Wa 'As-haabush-Shimaal,—maaa 'As-haabush-Shimaal?

42. Fii samuuminw-wa hamiim,—

43. Wa zillim-miny-yahmuum:

44. Laa baaridinw-wa laa kariim.

45. 'Innahum kaanuu qabla zaalika mutrafiin,
46. Wa kaanuu yusirruuna 'alal-hinsil-'aziim!
47. Wa kaanuu yaquuluuna, 'a-'izaa mitnaa wa kunnaa turaabanw-wa 'izaaman 'a-'innaa lamab-'uusuun,

48. 'Awa 'aabaaa-'unal-'awwa-luun?
49. Qul 'innal-'awwaliina wal-'aakhiriina,

---

38. For the Companions of the Right Hand.
39. A (goodly) number from those of old,
40. And a (goodly) number from those of later times.
41. The Companions of the Left Hand,—what will be the Companions of the Left Hand!
42. (They will be) in the midst of a fierce Blast of Fire and in Boiling Water,
43. And in the shades of Black Smoke:
44. Neither cool nor refreshing:
45. For that they were wont to be indulged, before that, in sinful luxury,
46. And persisted obstinately in wickedness supreme!
47. And they used to say, "What! when we die and become dust and bones, shall we then indeed be raised up again?—
48. "(We) and our fathers of old?"
49. Say: "Yea, those of old and those of later times,

50. Lamaj-muu-'uuna 'ilaa miiqaati Yawmim-ma'-luum.

51. Summa 'innakum 'ayyuhaz-zaaalluunal-mukazzibuun!

52. La-'aakiluuna min-Shajarim-min-Zaqquum.

53. Famaali-'uuna minhal-butuun,—

54. Fashaaribuuna 'alayhi minal-Hamiim:

55. Fashaaribuuna shurbal-hiim!

56. Haazaa nuzuluhum Yawmad-Diin!

57. Nahnu khalaqnaakum falaw-laa tusaddiquun?

58. 'Afara-'ay-tum-maa tumnuun?

59. 'A-'antum takhluquuna-huuu 'am Nahnul-Khaaliquun?

60. Nahnu qaddarnaa bay-na-kumul—Mawta wa maa Nahnu bimasbuuqiina

61. 'Alaaa 'an-nubaddila 'Am-saalakum wa nun-shi-'akum fii maa laa ta'-lamuun.

---

50. "All will certainly be gathered together for the meeting appointed for a Day well-known.

51. "Then will ye truly,— O ye that go wrong, and deny (the truth);

52. "Ye will surely taste of the Tree of Zaqqûm.

53. "Then will ye fill your insides therewith,

54. "And drink Boiling Water on top of it:

55. "Indeed ye shall drink Like diseased camels raging with thirst!"

56. Such will be their entertainment on the Day of Requital!

57. It is We Who have created you: why will ye not admit the Truth?

58. Do ye then see? the (human Seed) that ye emit,—

59. Is it ye who create it, or are We the Creators?

60. We have decreed Death to be your common lot, and We are not to be frustrated

61. From changing your Forms and creating you (again) in (Forms) that ye know not.

62. Wa laqad 'alimtumun-nash-'atal-'uulaa falaw laa tazak-karuun?

وَلَقَدْ عَلِمْتُمُ النَّشْأَةَ الْأُوْلٰى فَلَوْ لَا تَذَكَّرُوْنَ ۞

63. 'Afara-'aytum-maa tahrusuun?

أَفَرَءَيْتُمْ مَّا تَحْرُثُوْنَ ۞

64. 'A-'antum tazra-'uunahuuu 'am Nahnuz-zaari-'uun?

ءَأَنْتُمْ تَزْرَعُوْنَهُ أَمْ نَحْنُ الزَّارِعُوْنَ ۞

65. Law nashaaa-'u laja-'al-naahu hutaaman-fa-zal-tum tafakkahuun:

لَوْ نَشَآءُ لَجَعَلْنٰهُ حُطَامًا فَظَلْتُمْ تَفَكَّهُوْنَ ۞

66. 'Innaa lamugramuun:

إِنَّا لَمُغْرَمُوْنَ ۞

67. Bal nahnu mahruumuun.

بَلْ نَحْنُ مَحْرُوْمُوْنَ ۞

68. 'Afara-'ay-tumul-maaa-'al-lazii tashrabuun?

أَفَرَءَيْتُمُ الْمَآءَ الَّذِيْ تَشْرَبُوْنَ ۞

69. 'A-'antum 'anzal-tumuuhu minal-muzni 'am Nahnul-mun-ziluun?

ءَأَنْتُمْ أَنْزَلْتُمُوْهُ مِنَ الْمُزْنِ أَمْ نَحْنُ الْمُنْزِلُوْنَ ۞

70. Law nashaaa-'u ja-'alnaahu 'ujaajan-falaw laa tash-kuruun?

لَوْ نَشَآءُ جَعَلْنٰهُ أُجَاجًا فَلَوْ لَا تَشْكُرُوْنَ ۞

71. 'Afara-'ay-tumun-naaral-tatii tuuruun?

أَفَرَءَيْتُمُ النَّارَ الَّتِيْ تُوْرُوْنَ ۞

72. 'A-'antum 'ansha'-tum shajara-tahaaa 'am Nahnul-munshi-'uun?

ءَأَنْتُمْ أَنْشَأْتُمْ شَجَرَتَهَآ أَمْ نَحْنُ الْمُنْشِئُوْنَ ۞

73. Nahnu ja-'alnaahaa tazkiratanw-wa mataa-'al-lil-muq-wiin.

نَحْنُ جَعَلْنٰهَا تَذْكِرَةً وَّمَتَاعًا لِّلْمُقْوِيْنَ

---

62. And ye certainly know already the first form of creation: why then do ye not take heed?

63. See ye the seed that ye sow in the ground?

64. Is it ye that cause it to grow, or are We the Cause?

65. Were it Our Will, We could make it broken orts. And ye would be left in wonderment,

66. (Saying), "We are indeed Left with debts (for nothing):

67. "Indeed we are deprived".

68. See ye the water which ye drink?

69. Do ye bring it Down (in rain) from the Cloud or do We?

70. Were it Our Will, We could make it Saltish (and unpalatable): then why do ye not give thanks?

71. See ye the Fire which ye kindle?

72. Is it ye who grow the tree which feeds the fire, or do We grow it?

73. We have made it a reminder and an article of comfort and convenience for the denizens of deserts.

74. Fasabbih bismi-Rabbikal-'Aziim! (Part Three-fourth) (Section 3)

75. Falaaa 'uqsimu bimmawaaqi-'in-Nujuum,—

76. Wa 'innahuu laqasamul-law ta'-lamuuna 'aziim,—

77. 'Innahuu la-Qur-'aanun-Kariim

78. Fii Kitaabim-mak-nuun,—

79. Laa yamassuhuuu 'illal-mutahharuun:

80. Tanziilum-mir-Rabbil-'Aalamiin.

81. 'Afa-bi-haazal-Hadiisi 'antum-mud-hinuun?

82. Wa taj-'aluuna rizqakum 'annakum tukazzibuun?

83. Falaw laaa 'izaa balagatil-hulquum,—

84. Wa 'antum hiina-'izin-tanzuruun,—

85. Wa Nahnu 'aqrabu 'ilayhi minkum wa laakillaa tubsiruun,—

---

74. Then glorify the name of thy Lord, the Supreme!
75. Furthermore I swear by the setting of the Stars,—
76. And that is indeed a mighty adjuration if ye but knew,—
77. That this is indeed a Qur'ān most honourable,
78. In a Book well-guarded,
79. Which none shall touch but those who are clean:
80. A Revelation from the Lord of the Worlds.
81. Is it such a Message that ye would hold in light esteem?
82. And have ye made it your livelihood that ye should declare it false?
83. Then why do ye not (intervene) when (the soul of the dying man) reaches the throat,—
84. And ye the while (sit) looking on—
85. But We are nearer to him than ye, and yet see not,—

86. Falaw laaa 'in-kuntum gayra madiiniin,–

87. Tarji-'uunahaaa 'in-kuntum saadiqiin?

88. Fa-'ammaaa 'in-kaana minal-Muqarrabiina,–

89. Fa-Rawhunw-wa Ray-haanunw-wa Jannatu Na-'iim.

90. Wa 'ammaaa 'in-kaana min 'As-haabil-yamiin,–

91. Fa-Salaamul-laka min 'As-haabil-yamiin.

92. Wa 'ammaaa 'in-kaana minal-Mukazzibiinaz-zaaalliin,

93. Fanuzulum-min hamiim,–

94. Wa tas-liyatu Jahiim.

95. 'Inna haazaa lahuwa Haqqul-Yaqiin.

96. Fasabbih bismi Rabbikal-'Aziim.

---

86. Then why do ye not,— if you are exempt from (future) account,—

87. Call back the soul, if ye are tr-ue (in your claim of Independence)?

88. Thus then, if he be of those Nearest to Allah,

89. (There is for him) Rest and Satisfaction, and a Garden of Delights.

90. And if he be of the Companions of the Right Hand,

91. (For him is the salutation), "Peace be unto thee,'' from the Companions of the Right Hand.

92. And if he be of those who deny (the truth) who go wrong,

93. For him is Entertainment with Boiling Water,

94. And burning in Hell-Fire.

95. Verily, this is the very Truth of assured Certainty.

96. So glorify the name of thy Lord, the Supreme.

Mulk–67
Verses 30–Sections 2

Bismillaahir-Raḥmaanir-Raḥiim.

1. TABAARAKALLAZII bi-Yadihil-MULK; wa Huwa 'alaa kulli shay-'in-Qadiir:–

2. 'Allazii khalaqal-Mawta wal-Hayaata li-yabluwakum 'ayyukum 'ahsanu 'amalaa: wa Huwal-'Aziizul-Gafuur;–

3. 'Allazii khalaqa sab-'a samaawaatiñ-ṭibaaqaa: maa taraa fii Khalqir-Raḥmaani miñ-tafaa-wut. Farji-'il-basara hal taraa min-futuur?

4. Summar-ji-'il-basara kar-ratayni yañqalib 'ilaykal-baṣaru khaasi-'añw-wa huwa hasiir.

5. Wa laqad zayyannas-samaaa-'addunyaa bimaṣaabiiḥa wa ja-'alnaahaa rujuumal-lish-shayaaṭiini wa 'a'-tadnaa la-hum 'azaabas- Sa-'iir.

Al-Mulk, or Dominion

In the name of Allah, Most Gracious, Most Merciful.

1. Blessed be He in Whose hands is Dominion; and He over all things hath Power;—

2. He Who created Death and Life, that He may try which of you is best in deed: and He is the Exalted in Might, Oft-Forgiving;—

3. He Who created the seven heavens one above another: no want of proportion wilt thou see in the Creation of The Most Gracious. So turn thy vision again: seest thou any flaw?

4. Again turn thy vision a second time: (thy) vision will come back to thee dull and discomfited, in a state worn out.

5. And We have, (from of old), adorned the lowest heaven with Lamps, and We have made such (Lamps) (as) missiles to drive away Satans, and have prepared for them the Chastisement of the Blazing Fire.

6. Wa lillaziina kafaruu bi-Rabbihim 'Azaaba Jahannam: wa bi'-sal-masiir.

7. 'Izaaa 'ulquu fiihaa sami-'uu lahaa shahiiqanw-wa hiya tafuur,—

8. Takaadu tamayyazu minal-gayz̧: kullamaaa 'ulqiya fiihaa fawjun sa-'alahum khazanatu-haaa 'alam ya'-tikum Naẓiir?

9. Qaaluu balaa qad jaaa-'anaa Naẓiir; fakaẓẓabnaa wa qulnaa maa nazzalallaahu min-shay': 'in 'antum 'illaa fii ẓalaalin-kabiir!

10. Wa qaaluu law kunnaa nasma-'u 'aw na'-qilu maa kunnaa fiii 'Aṣ-ḥaabis-Sa-'iir!

11. Fa'-tarafuu bi-ẕambihim: fasuḥ-qal-li-'Aṣ-ḥaabis-Sa-'iir!

---

6. For those who reject their Lord (and Cherisher) is the Chastisement of Hell: and evil is (such) destination.

7. When they are cast therein, they will hear the (terrible) drawing in of its breath even as it blazes forth.

8. Almost bursting with fury: every time a Group will ask, is cast therein, its Keepers will ask, "Did no Warner come to you?"

9. They will say: "Yes indeed; a Warner did come to us, but we rejected him and said, 'Allah never sent down any (Message): ye are in nothing but a grave error' !"

10. They will further say: "Had we but listened or used our intelligence we should not (now) be among the Companions of the Blazing Fire!"

11. They will then confess their sins: but far from Allah's mercy are the Companions of the Blazing Fire!

12. 'Innallaẓiina yakh-shawna Rabbahum-bil-gaybi lahum-Magfiratuňw-wa 'Ajruň-kabiir.

إِنَّ الَّذِيْنَ يَخْشَوْنَ رَبَّهُمْ بِالْغَيْبِ لَهُمْ مَّغْفِرَةٌ وَّأَجْرٌ كَبِيْرٌ ۞

13. Wa 'asirruu qawlakum 'awij-haruu bih; 'innahuu 'Aliimum-bizaatis-suduur.

وَأَسِرُّوْا قَوْلَكُمْ أَوِ اجْهَرُوْا بِهِ ۖ إِنَّهُ عَلِيْمٌۢ بِذَاتِ الصُّدُوْرِ ۞

14. 'Alaa ya'-lamu man khalaq? Wa Huwal-Laṭiiful-Khabiir. (Section 4)

أَلَا يَعْلَمُ مَنْ خَلَقَ ۖ وَهُوَ اللَّطِيْفُ الْخَبِيْرُ ۞

15. Huwallaẓii ja-'ala lakumul-'arẓa zaluulaň-famshuu fii manaakibihaa wa kuluu mir-Rizqih: wa 'ilay-hin-Nushuur.

هُوَ الَّذِيْ جَعَلَ لَكُمُ الْأَرْضَ ذَلُوْلًا فَامْشُوْا فِيْ مَنَاكِبِهَا وَكُلُوْا مِنْ رِّزْقِهِ ۖ وَإِلَيْهِ النُّشُوْرُ ۞

16. 'A-'amiňtum-maň-fis-Samaaa-'i 'aňy-yakh-sifa bi-kumul-'arẓa fa-'iẓaa hiya tamuur?

ءَأَمِنْتُمْ مَّنْ فِي السَّمَآءِ أَنْ يَّخْسِفَ بِكُمُ الْأَرْضَ فَإِذَا هِيَ تَمُوْرُ ۞

17. 'Am-'amiňtum-maň-fis-Samaaa-'i 'aňy-yursila 'alay-kum haaṣibaa? Fasata'-lamuuna kayfa naẓiir.

أَمْ أَمِنْتُمْ مَّنْ فِي السَّمَآءِ أَنْ يُّرْسِلَ عَلَيْكُمْ حَاصِبًا ۖ فَسَتَعْلَمُوْنَ كَيْفَ نَذِيْرِ ۞

---

12. As for those who fear their Lord unseen for them is Forgiveness and a great Reward.

13. And whether ye hide your word or make it known, He certainly has (full) knowledge, of the secrets of (all) hearts.

14. Should He not know,—He that created? And He is the Subtle the Aware.

15. It is He Who has made the earth manageable for you, so traverse ye through its tracts and enjoy of the Sustenance which He furnishes: but unto Him is the Resurrection.

16. Do ye feel secure that He Who is in Heaven will not cause you to be swallowed up by the earth when it shakes (as in an earthquake) ?

17. Or do ye feel secure that He Who is in Heaven will not send against you a violent tornado (with showers of stones), so that ye shall know how (terrible) was My warning?

18. Wa laqad kazzaballaziina min-qablihim fa-kay-fa kaana nakiir?

وَلَقَدْ كَذَّبَ الَّذِيْنَ مِنْ قَبْلِهِمْ فَكَيْفَ كَانَ نَكِيْرِ ۞

19. 'Awalam yaraw 'ilat-tayri fawqahum saaffaatinw-wa yaqbizn? Maa yumsiku-hunna 'illar-Rahmaan: 'innahuu bi-kulli shay-'im-Basiir.

أَوَلَمْ يَرَوْا إِلَى الطَّيْرِ فَوْقَهُمْ صٰۤفّٰتٍ وَّيَقْبِضْنَ مَا يُمْسِكُهُنَّ إِلَّا الرَّحْمٰنُ إِنَّهُ بِكُلِّ شَيْءٍ بَصِيْرٌ ۞

20. 'Amman haazallazii huwa jundul-lakum yansurukum-min duunir-Rahmaan? 'Inil-kaafi-ruuna 'illaa fii guruur.

أَمَّنْ هٰذَا الَّذِيْ هُوَ جُنْدٌ لَّكُمْ يَنْصُرُكُمْ مِنْ دُوْنِ الرَّحْمٰنِ إِنِ الْكٰفِرُوْنَ إِلَّا فِيْ غُرُوْرٍ ۞

21. 'Amman haazallazii yar-zuqukum 'in 'amsaka Rizqah? Bal-lajjuu fii 'utuwwiñw-wa nufuur.

أَمَّنْ هٰذَا الَّذِيْ يَرْزُقُكُمْ إِنْ أَمْسَكَ رِزْقَهُ بَلْ لَّجُّوْا فِيْ عُتُوٍّ وَّنُفُوْرٍ ۞

22. 'Afamañy-yamshii mukibban 'alaa wajhihiii 'ahdaaa 'ammañy-yamshii sa-wiyyan 'alaa Siraatim-Mustaqiim.

أَفَمَنْ يَّمْشِيْ مُكِبًّا عَلٰى وَجْهِهٖ أَهْدٰى أَمَّنْ يَّمْشِيْ سَوِيًّا عَلٰى صِرَاطٍ مُّسْتَقِيْمٍ ۞

---

18. But indeed men before them rejected (My warning): then how (terrible) was My punishment (of them)?

19. Do they not observe the birds above them, spreading their wings and folding them in ? None can uphold them except The Most Gracious: truly it is He that watches over all things.

20. Nay, who is there that can help you, (even as) an army, besides The Most Merciful ? In nothing but delusion are the Unbelievers.

21. Or who is there that can provide you with Sustenance if He were to withhold His provision? Nay, they obstinately persist in insolent impiety and flight (from the Truth).

22. Is then one who walks headlong, with his face grovelling, better guided,—or one who walks evenly on a Straight Way ?

23. Qul Huwallaziii 'ansha-'akum wa ja-'ala lakumus-sam-'a wal-'abṣaara wal-'af-'idah: qaliilam-maa tash-kuruun.

قُلْ هُوَالَّذِيٓ اَنْشَاَكُمْ وَجَعَلَ لَكُمُ السَّمْعَ وَالْاَبْصَارَ وَالْاَفْـِٔدَةَ ۭ قَلِيْلًا مَّا تَشْكُرُوْنَ ۝

24. Qul Huwallazii zara-'akum fil-'arzi wa 'ilay-hi tuḥ-sharuun.

قُلْ هُوَالَّذِيْ ذَرَاَكُمْ فِى الْاَرْضِ وَ اِلَيْهِ تُحْشَرُوْنَ ۝

25. Wa yaquuluuna mataa haazal-wa'-du 'in-kuntum ṣaadiqiin.

وَيَقُوْلُوْنَ مَتٰى هٰذَا الْوَعْدُ اِنْ كُنْتُمْ صٰدِقِيْنَ ۝

26. Qul 'innamal-'ilmu 'indal-laah: wa 'innamaaa 'ana Naẓiirum-mubiin.

قُلْ اِنَّمَا الْعِلْمُ عِنْدَ اللّٰهِ ۠ وَاِنَّمَآ اَنَا نَذِيْرٌ مُّبِيْنٌ ۝

27. Falammaa ra-'awhu zul-fatañ-siii-'at wujuuhullaziina kafaruu wa qiila haazallazii kuntum-bihii tadda-'uun!

فَلَمَّا رَاَوْهُ زُلْفَةً سِيْٓـَٔتْ وُجُوْهُ الَّذِيْنَ كَفَرُوْا وَقِيْلَ هٰذَا الَّذِيْ كُنْتُمْ بِهٖ تَدَّعُوْنَ ۝

28. Qul 'ara-'aytum 'in 'ah-lakani-yallaahu wa mamma-'iya 'aw rahimanaa famañy-yujiirul-kaafiriina min 'Aẓaabin 'aliim.

قُلْ اَرَءَيْتُمْ اِنْ اَهْلَكَنِىَ اللّٰهُ وَمَنْ مَّعِىَ اَوْ رَحِمَنَا ۙ فَمَنْ يُّجِيْرُ الْكٰفِرِيْنَ مِنْ عَذَابٍ اَلِيْمٍ ۝

---

23. Say: "It is He Who has created you, and made for you the faculties of hearing, seeing, and understanding: little thanks it is ye give.

24. Say: "It is He Who has multiplied you through the earth, and to Him shall ye be gathered together."

25. They ask: When will this promise be (fulfilled)? If ye are telling the truth.

26. Say: "As to the knowledge of the time, it is with Allah alone: I am a plain warner."

27. At length, when they see it close at hand, grieved will be the faces of the Unbelievers, and it will be said (to them): "This is (the promise fulfilled) which ye were calling for !"

28. Say: "See ye ?—If Allah were to destroy me, and those with me, or if He bestows his Mercy on us,— yet who can deliver the Unbelievers from a grievous Chastisement ?

29. Qul Huwar-Raḥmaanu 'aamannaa bihii wa 'alay-hi ta-wakkal-naa: fasata'-lamuuna man huwa fii zalaalim-mubiin.

قُلْ هُوَ الرَّحْمٰنُ اٰمَنَّا بِهٖ وَعَلَيْهِ تَوَكَّلْنَا ۚ فَسَتَعْلَمُوْنَ مَنْ هُوَ فِيْ ضَلٰلٍ مُّبِيْنٍ ۝

30. Qul 'ara-'aytum 'in 'aṣbaḥa maaa-'ukum gaw-ran-famany-ya'-tiiikum-bi-maaa-'imma-'iin?

قُلْ اَرَءَيْتُمْ اِنْ اَصْبَحَ مَآؤُكُمْ غَوْرًا فَمَنْ يَّأْتِيْكُمْ بِمَآءٍ مَّعِيْنٍ ۝

---

29. Say: "He is The most Gracious: we have believed in Him, and on Him have we put our trust: so, soon will ye know which (of us) it is that is in manifest error."

30. Say. "See ye ?— If your stream be some morning lost (in the underground earth), who then can supply you with clear-flowing water?"

Nuuh—71
Verses 28–Sections 2

Bismillaahir-Raḥmaanir-Raḥiim.

1. 'Innaaa 'arsalnaa Nuuḥan 'ilaa Qawmihiii 'an 'anẓir Qawmaka min-qabli 'any-ya'-tiyahum 'Aẓaabun 'aliim.

2. Qaala yaa-Qawmi 'innii la-kum Naẓiirum-mubiin:

3. 'Ani'-budullaaha wattaquuhu wa 'aṭii-'uun:

4. Yagfir lakum-min-ẓunuubi-kum wa yu-'akhkhirkum 'ilaaa 'Ajalim-Musammaa: 'inna 'Ajalallaahi 'iẓaa jaaa-'a laa yu-'akhkhar. Law kuntum ta'-lamuun.

5. Qaala Rabbi 'innii da-'awtu Qawmii lay-lanw-wa nahaaraa:

Nûh, or Noah

In the name of Allah, Most Gracious, Most Merciful.

1. We sent Noah to his People (with the Command): "Do thou warn thy People before there comes to them a grievous Chastisement."

2. He said: "O my People ! I am to you a Warner, clear and open:

3. "That ye should worship Allah, fear Him, and obey me:

4. "So He may forgive you your sins and give you respite for a stated Term: for when the Term given by Allah is accomplished, it cannot be put forward: if ye only knew."

5. He said: "O my Lord ! I have called to my People night and day:

6.   Falam yazid-hum du-'aaa-'iii 'illaa firaaraa.

7.   Wa 'innii kullamaa da-'awtuhum li-tagfira lahum ja-'aluuu 'asaabi-'ahum fii 'aazaanihim was-tag-shaw siyaabahum wa 'asarruu was-tak-barus-tikbaaraa.

8.   Summa 'innii da-'awtuhum jihaaraa;

9.   Summa 'inniii 'a'-lantu lahum wa 'asrartu lahum 'israaraa,

10.   Faqul-tus-tagfiruu Rabbakum; 'innahuu kaana Gaffaaraa;

11.   Yursilis-samaaa-'a 'alay-kum-midraaraa;

12.   Wa yumdidkum-bi-'amwaa-liñw-wabaniinawayaj-'al-lakum Jan-naatiñw-wa yaj-'al-lakum 'anhaaraa.

13.   Maa lakum laa tarjuuna lillaahi waqaaraa,–

14.   Wa   qad   khalaqakum 'atwaaraa?

---

6.   "But my call only increases (their) flight (from the Right).

7.   "And every time I have called to them, that Thou mightest forgive them, they have (only) thrust their fingers into their ears, covered themselves up with their garments, grown obstinate, and given themselves up to arrogance.

8.   "So I have called to them aloud;

9.   "Further I have spoken to them in public and secretly in private,

10.   "Saying, 'Ask forgiveness from your Lord, for He is Oft-Forgiving;

11.   " 'He will send rain to you in abundance;

12.   " 'Give you increase in wealth and sons; and bestow on you gardens and bestow on you rivers (of flowing water).

13.   " 'What is the matter with you, that ye are not conscious of Allah's majesty,—

14.   " 'Seeing that it is He that has created you in diverse stages ?

15. 'Alam taraw kayfa khalaqallaahu sab-'a samaawaatin ṭibaaqaa. أَلَمْ تَرَوْا كَيْفَ خَلَقَ اللَّهُ سَبْعَ سَمٰوٰتٍ طِبَاقًا ۞

16. Wa ja-'alal-qamara fiihinna nuuranw-wa ja-'alash-shamsa Siraajaa? وَجَعَلَ الْقَمَرَ فِيهِنَّ نُوْرًا وَّجَعَلَ الشَّمْسَ سِرَاجًا ۞

17. Wallaahu 'ambatakum-minal-'arẓi nabaataa, وَاللَّهُ أَنْبَتَكُمْ مِّنَ الْأَرْضِ نَبَاتًا ۞

18. Ṣumma yu-'iidukum fiihaa wa yukhrijukum 'ikhraajaa? ثُمَّ يُعِيْدُكُمْ فِيْهَا وَيُخْرِجُكُمْ إِخْرَاجًا ۞

19. Wallaahu ja-'alalakumul-'arẓa bisaataa, وَاللَّهُ جَعَلَ لَكُمُ الْأَرْضَ بِسَاطًا ۞

20. Litaslukuu minhaa subulan-fijaajaa. (Section 2) لِّتَسْلُكُوْا مِنْهَا سُبُلًا فِجَاجًا ۞

21. Qaala Nuuḥur-Rabbi 'innahum 'aṣawnii wattaba-'uu mallam yazidhu maaluhuu wa waladuhuuu 'illaa khasaaraa. قَالَ نُوْحٌ رَّبِّ إِنَّهُمْ عَصَوْنِيْ وَاتَّبَعُوْا مَنْ لَّمْ يَزِدْهُ مَالُهُ وَوَلَدُهُ إِلَّا خَسَارًا ۞

22. Wa makaruu Makran-kubbaaraa. وَمَكَرُوْا مَكْرًا كُبَّارًا ۞

23. Wa qaaluu laa taẓarunna 'aalihatakum wa laa taẓarunna Waddanw-wa laa Suwaa-'aa, wa laa Yaguuṣa wa Ya-'uuqa wa Nasraa;– وَقَالُوْا لَا تَذَرُنَّ آلِهَتَكُمْ وَلَا تَذَرُنَّ وَدًّا وَّلَا سُوَاعًا وَّلَا يَغُوْثَ وَيَعُوْقَ وَنَسْرًا ۞

---

15. " 'See ye not how Allah has created the seven heavens one above another,

16. " 'And made the moon a light in their midst, and made the sun as a (Glorious) Lamp?

17. " 'And Allah has produced you from the earth, growing (gradually),

18. " 'And in the End He will return you into the (earth), and raise you forth (again at the Resurrection) ?

19. " 'And Allah has made the earth for you as a carpet (spread out),

20. " 'That ye may go about therein, in spacious roads.'

21. Noah said: "O my Lord! they have disobeyed me, but they follow (men) whose wealth and children give them no Increase but only Loss.

22. "And they have devised a tremendous Plot.

23. "And they have said (to each other), 'Abandon not your gods: abandon neither Wadd nor Suwa', neither Yagûth nor Ya'ûq, nor Nasr';——

24. Wa qad 'azalluu kasiiraa; wa laa tazidiz-zaalimiina 'illaa zalaalaa.

وَقَدْ اَضَلُّوْا كَثِيْرًا ۚ وَلَا تَزِدِ الظّٰلِمِيْنَ اِلَّا ضَلٰلًا ۝

25. Mimmaa khatiii-'aatihim 'ugriquu fa-'ud-khiluu Naaraa: falam yajiduu lahum-min-duu-nillaahi 'ansaaraa.

مِمَّا خَطِيْٓئٰتِهِمْ اُغْرِقُوْا فَاُدْخِلُوْا نَارًا ۙ فَلَمْ يَجِدُوْا لَهُمْ مِّنْ دُوْنِ اللهِ اَنْصَارًا ۝

26. Wa qaala Nuuhur-Rabbi laa tazar 'alal-'arzi minal-kaafiriina dayyaaraa!

وَقَالَ نُوْحٌ رَّبِّ لَا تَذَرْ عَلَى الْاَرْضِ مِنَ الْكٰفِرِيْنَ دَيَّارًا ۝

27. 'Innaka 'in-tazarhum yuzilluu 'ibaadaka wa laa yaliduuu 'illaa faajiran-kaffaaraa.

اِنَّكَ اِنْ تَذَرْهُمْ يُضِلُّوْا عِبَادَكَ وَلَا يَلِدُوْٓا اِلَّا فَاجِرًا كَفَّارًا ۝

28. Rabbig-fir lii wa liwaalidayya wa liman-dakhala baytiya Mu'-minanw-wa lil-Mu'-miniina wal-Mu'-minaat: wa laa tazidiz-zaalimiina 'illaa tabaaraa!
(Part One Half)

رَبِّ اغْفِرْ لِيْ وَلِوَالِدَيَّ وَلِمَنْ دَخَلَ بَيْتِيَ مُؤْمِنًا وَّلِلْمُؤْمِنِيْنَ وَالْمُؤْمِنٰتِ ۚ وَلَا تَزِدِ الظّٰلِمِيْنَ اِلَّا تَبَارًا ۝

---

24. "They have already misled many; and grant Thou no increase to the wrong-doers but in straying (from their mark)."

25. Because of their sins they were drowned (in the flood), and were made to enter the Fire and they found— in lieu of Allah— none to help them.

26. And Noah said: "O my Lord ! Leave not of the Unbelievers, a single one on earth !

27. "For, if Thou dost leave (any of) them, they will but mislead Thy devotees, and they will breed none but wicked ungrateful ones.

28. "O my Lord ! Forgive me, my parents, all who enter my house in Faith, and (all) believing men and believing women: and to the wrong-doers grant Thou no increase but in Perdition !"

Jinn—72
Verses 28—Sections 2

Bismillaahir-Rahmaanir-Rahiim.

1. Qul 'uuhiya 'ilayya 'anna-hustama-'a nafarum-minal-Jinni faqaaluuu 'innaa sami'-naa Qur-'aanan 'ajabaa,

2. Yahdiii 'ilar-Rushdi fa-'aa-mannaa bih: wa lan-nushrika bi-Rabbinaaa 'ahadaa.

3. Wa 'annahuu Ta-'aalaa Jaddu Rabbinaa mattakhaza saa-hibatanw-wa laa waladaa.

4. Wa 'annahuu kaana yaquulu safiihunaa 'alallaahi shatataa;

5. Wa 'annaa zanannaaa 'allan-taquulal-'insu wal-jinnu 'alal-laahi kazibaa.

6. Wa 'annahuu kaana rijaalum-minal-'insi ya-'uuzuuna bi-rijaalim-minal-Jinni fazaaduu-hum rahaqaa.

Al-Jinn, The Jinn

In the name of Allah, Most Gracious, Most Merciful.

1. Say: It has been revealed to me that a company of Jinns listened (to the Qur-ān). They said, 'We have really heard a wonderful Recital!

2. 'It gives guidance to the Right, and we have believed therein: we shall not join (in worship) any (gods) with our Lord,

3. 'And exalted is the Majesty of our Lord: He has taken neither a wife nor a son.

4. 'There were some foolish ones among us, who used to utter extravagant lies against Allah;

5. 'But we do think that no man or jinn should say aught that is untrue against Allah.

6. 'True, there were persons among mankind who took shelter with persons among the Jinns, but they increased them into further error.

7. Wa 'annahum zannuu kamaa zanantum 'allany-yab-'asal-laahu 'ahadaa.

وَّاَنَّهُمْ ظَنُّوْا كَمَا ظَنَنْتُمْ اَنْ لَّنْ يَّبْعَثَ اللّٰهُ اَحَدًا ۞

8. Wa 'annaa lamasnas-samaaa-'a fawajadnaahaa muli-'at harasan-shadiidanw-wa shuhubaa.

وَّاَنَّا لَمَسْنَا السَّمَآءَ فَوَجَدْنٰهَا مُلِئَتْ حَرَسًا شَدِيْدًا وَّشُهُبًا ۞

9. Wa 'annaa kunnaa naq-'udu minhaa maqaa-'ida lis-sam'; famany-yastami-'il-'aana yajid lahuu shihaabar-rasadaa.

وَّاَنَّا كُنَّا نَقْعُدُ مِنْهَا مَقَاعِدَ لِلسَّمْعِ ۙ فَمَنْ يَّسْتَمِعِ الْاٰنَ يَجِدْ لَهٗ شِهَابًا رَّصَدًا ۞

10. Wa 'annaa laa nadriii 'a-sharrun 'uriida biman-fil-'arzi 'am 'araada bihim Rab-buhum rashadaa.

وَّاَنَّا لَا نَدْرِيْٓ اَشَرٌّ اُرِيْدَ بِمَنْ فِى الْاَرْضِ اَمْ اَرَادَ بِهِمْ رَبُّهُمْ رَشَدًا ۞

11. Wa 'annaa minnas-saali-huuna wa minnaa duuna zaalik: kunnaa taraaa-'iqa qidadaa.

وَّاَنَّا مِنَّا الصّٰلِحُوْنَ وَمِنَّا دُوْنَ ذٰلِكَ ۖ كُنَّا طَرَآئِقَ قِدَدًا ۞

12. Wa 'annaa zanannaaa 'allan-nu'-jizallaaha fil-'arzi wa lan-nu'-jizahuu harabaa.

وَّاَنَّا ظَنَنَّآ اَنْ لَّنْ نُّعْجِزَ اللّٰهَ فِى الْاَرْضِ وَلَنْ نُّعْجِزَهٗ هَرَبًا ۞

---

7. 'And they (came to) think as ye thought, that Allah would not raise up anyone (to Judgment).

8. 'And we pried into the (secrets of) heaven; but we found it filled with stern guards and flaming fires.

9. 'We used, indeed, to sit there in (hidden) stations, to (steal) a hearing; but any who listens now will find a flaming fire watching him in ambush.

10. 'And we understand not whether ill is intended to those on earth on whether their Lord (really) intends to guide them to right conduct.

11. 'There are among us some that are righteous, and some the contrary: we follow divergent paths.

12. 'But we think that we can by no means frustrate Allah throughout the earth, nor can we escape Him by flight.

13. Wa 'annaa lammaa sami'-nal-Hudaaa 'aamannaa bih. Famany-yu'-mim-bi-Rabbihii falaa yakhaafu bakhsanwwa laa rahaqaa.

وَّ اَنَّا لَمَّا سَمِعْنَا الْهُدٰى اٰمَنَّا بِهٖ فَمَنْ يُّؤْمِنْ بِرَبِّهٖ فَلَا يَخَافُ بَخْسًا وَّ لَا رَهَقًا ۞

14. Wa 'annaa minnal-Muslimuuna wa minnal-Qaasituun. Faman 'aslama fa-'ulaaa-'ika taharraw rashadaa.

وَّ اَنَّا مِنَّا الْمُسْلِمُوْنَ وَ مِنَّا الْقَاسِطُوْنَ فَمَنْ اَسْلَمَ فَاُولٰٓئِكَ تَحَرَّوْا رَشَدًا ۞

15. Wa 'ammal-Qaasituuna fakaanuu li-Jahannama hatabaa--

وَ اَمَّا الْقَاسِطُوْنَ فَكَانُوْا لِجَهَنَّمَ حَطَبًا ۞

16. Wa 'alla-wis-taqaamuu 'alat-Tariiqati la-'asqaynaa-hum-maaa-'an gadaqaa.

وَّ اَنْ لَّوِ اسْتَقَامُوْا عَلَى الطَّرِيْقَةِ لَاَسْقَيْنٰهُمْ مَّاءً غَدَقًا ۞

17. Linaftinahum fiih. Wa many-yu'-riz 'an Zikri Rabbihii yasluk-hu 'Azaabañ-sa-'adaa.

لِنَفْتِنَهُمْ فِيْهِ وَ مَنْ يُّعْرِضْ عَنْ ذِكْرِ رَبِّهٖ يَسْلُكْهُ عَذَابًا صَعَدًا ۞

18. Wa 'annal-Masaajida lillaahi falaa tad-'uu ma-'allaahi 'ahadaa;

وَّ اَنَّ الْمَسٰجِدَ لِلّٰهِ فَلَا تَدْعُوْا مَعَ اللّٰهِ اَحَدًا ۞

---

13. 'And as for us, since we have listened to the Guidance, we have accepted it: and any who believes in his Lord has no fear, either of a short (account) or of any injustice.

14. 'Amongst us are some that submit their wills (to Allah), and some that swerve from justice. Now those who submit their wills—they have sought out (the path) of right conduct:

15. 'But those who swerve,— they are (but) fuel for Hell-fire'—

16. (And Allah's Message is): "If they (the Pagans) had (only) remained on the (right) Way, We should certainly have bestowed on them Rain in abundance.

17. "That We might try them by that (means). But if any turns away from the remembrance of his Lord, He will cause him to undergo ever-growing Chastisement.

18. "And the places of worship are for Allah (alone): so invoke not anyone along with Allah;

19. Wa 'annahuu lammaa qaama 'Abdullaahi yad-'uuhu kaaduu yakuunuuna 'alay-hi libadaa. (Section 2)

20. Qul 'innamaaa 'ad-'uu Rabbii wa laaa 'ushriku bihiii 'ahadaa.

21. Qul 'innii laaa 'amliku lakum zarranw-wa laa rashadaa.

22. Qul 'innii lany-yujiiranii minallaahi 'ahad, wa lan 'ajida min-duunihii mul-tahadaa,

23. 'Illaa balaagam-minallaahi wa Risaalaatih: wa many-ya'-sillaaha wa Rasuulahuu fa-'inna lahuu Naara Jahannama khaalidiina fiihaaa 'abadaa.

24. Hattaaa 'izaa ra-'aw maa yuu-'aduuna fasaya'-lamuuna man 'az-'afu naasiranw-wa 'aqallu 'adadaa.

---

19. "Yet when the Devotees of Allah stood up to invoke Him, they just make round-him a dense crowd."

20. Say: "I do no more than invoke my Lord, and I join not with Him any (false god)."

21. Say: "It is not in my power to cause you harm, or to bring you to right conduct."

22. Say: "No one can deliver me from Allah (if I were to disobey Him), nor should I find refuge except in Him,

23. "Unless I deliver what I receive from Allah and His Messages: for any that disobey Allah and His Messenger,—for them is Hell: they shall dwell therein for ever."

24. At length, when they see (with their own eyes) that which they are promised,— then will they know who it is that is weakest in (his) helper and least important in point of numbers.

25. Qul 'in 'adriii 'a-qariibum-maa tuu-'aduuna 'am yaj-'alu lahuu Rabbiii 'amadaa.

قُلْ اِنْ اَدْرِيٓ اَقَرِيْبٌ مَّا تُوْعَدُوْنَ اَمْ يَجْعَلُ لَهُ رَبِّيٓ اَمَدًا ۝

26. 'Aalimul-Gaybi falaa yuẓhiru 'alaa Gaybihiii 'aḥadaa,

عٰلِمُ الْغَيْبِ فَلَا يُظْهِرُ عَلٰى غَيْبِهٖٓ اَحَدًا ۝

27. 'Illaa manirtaẓaa mir-ra-suulin-fa-'innahuu yas-luku mim-bayni yadayhi wa min khalfihii raṣadaa,

اِلَّا مَنِ ارْتَضٰى مِنْ رَّسُوْلٍ فَاِنَّهُ يَسْلُكُ مِنْۢ بَيْنِ يَدَيْهِ وَمِنْ خَلْفِهٖ رَصَدًا ۝

28. Liya'-lama 'an-qad 'ablaguu Risaalaati Rabbihim wa 'aḥaata bimaa laday-him wa 'aḥṣaa kulla shay-'in 'adadaa.

لِيَعْلَمَ اَنْ قَدْ اَبْلَغُوْا رِسٰلٰتِ رَبِّهِمْ وَاَحَاطَ بِمَا لَدَيْهِمْ وَاَحْصٰى كُلَّ شَيْءٍ عَدَدًا ۝

---

25. Say: "I know not whether the (Punishment) which ye are promised is near, or whether my Lord will appoint for it a distant term.

26. "He (alone) knows the Unseen, nor does He make anyone acquainted with His Secrets.—

27. "Except a messenger whom He has chosen: and then He makes a band of watchers march before him and behind him,

28. "That He may know that they have (truly) brought and delivered the Messages of their Lord and He encompasses all that is with them, and takes account of every single thing."

Muzzammil–73
Verses 20–Sections 2

Bismillaahir-Rahmaanir-Rahiim.

سُوْرَةُ الْمُزَّمِّلِ مَكِّيَّةٌ وَّهِىَ عِشْرُوْنَ اٰيَةً وَّفِيْهَا رُكُوْعَانِ

بِسْمِ اللهِ الرَّحْمٰنِ الرَّحِيْمِ

1. Yaaa-'ayyuhal-MUZZAMMIL!

يٰۤاَيُّهَا الْمُزَّمِّلُ ۙ ۱

2. Qumil-layla 'illaa qaliilaa,--

قُمِ الَّيْلَ اِلَّا قَلِيْلًا ۙ ۲

3. Nisfahuuu 'a-winqus-minhu qaliilaa,

نِّصْفَهٗۤ اَوِ انْقُصْ مِنْهُ قَلِيْلًا ۙ ۳

4. 'Aw zid 'alayhi wa rattilil-Qur-'aana tartiilaa.

اَوْ زِدْ عَلَيْهِ وَرَتِّلِ الْقُرْاٰنَ تَرْتِيْلًا ۙ ۴

5. 'Innaa sanulqii 'alayka Qawlan-saqiilaa.

اِنَّا سَنُلْقِيْ عَلَيْكَ قَوْلًا ثَقِيْلًا ۵

6. 'Inna naashi-'atal-layli hiya 'ashaddu wat-'anw-wa 'aqwamu Qiilaa.

اِنَّ نَاشِئَةَ الَّيْلِ هِىَ اَشَدُّ وَطْاً وَّاَقْوَمُ قِيْلًا ۷

7. 'Inna laka fin-nahaari sabhan-tawiilaa.

اِنَّ لَكَ فِى النَّهَارِ سَبْحًا طَوِيْلًا ۸

8. Wazkurisma Rabbika wa tabattal 'ilayhi tabtiilaa.

وَاذْكُرِ اسْمَ رَبِّكَ وَتَبَتَّلْ اِلَيْهِ تَبْتِيْلًا ۸

Al-Muzzammil, or Folded in Garments

In the name of Allah, Most Gracious, Most Merciful.

1. O thou folded in garments !
2. Stand (to prayer) by night, but not all night—
3. Half of it,— or a little less,
4. Or a little more; and recite the Qur'ān in slow, measured rhythmic tones.
5. Soon shall We send down to thee a weighty Word.
6. Truly the rising by night is a time when impression is more keen and speech more certain.
7. True, there is for thee by day prolonged occupation with ordinary duties:
8. But keep in remembrance the name of thy Lord, and devote thyself to Him whole-heartedly.

9. Rabbul-Mashriqi wal-Magribi Laaa 'ilaaha 'illaa Huwa fattakhiz-hu Wakiilaa.

10. Wasbir 'alaa maa yaquuluuna wah-jurhum hajran-jamiilaa.

11. Wa zarnii wal-mukazzi-biina 'ulin-na'-mati wa mahhil-hum qaliilaa.

12. 'Inna ladaynaaa 'ankaa-lanw-wa Jahiimaa,

13. Wa Ta-'aaman-zaa gussa-tinw-wa 'Azaaban 'aliimaa.

14. Yawma tarjuful-'arzu wal-jibaalu wa kaanatil-jibaalu kasiibam-mahiilaa.

15. 'Innaaa 'arsalnaaa 'ilaykum Rasuulan-shaahidan 'alaykum kamaaa 'arsalnaaa 'ilaa Fir-'awna Rasuulaa.

---

9. (He is) Lord of the East and the West: there is no god but He: take Him therefore for (thy) Disposer of Affairs.

10. And have patience with what they say, and leave them with noble (dignity).

11. And leave Me (alone to deal with) those in possession of the good things of life (who (yet) deny the Truth;) and bear with them for a little while.

12. With Us are Fetters (to bind them), and a Fire (to burn them),

13. And a Food that chokes and a Chastisement Grievous.

14. The Day the earth and the mountains will be in violent commotion. And the mountains will be as a heap of sand poured out and flowing down.

15. We have sent to you, (O men!) a Messenger, to be a witness concerning you even as We sent a messenger to Pharaoh.

16. Fa-'asaa Fir-'awnur-Rasuula fa-'akhaznaahu 'akhzañw-wabiilaa.

17. Fakay-fa tattaquuna 'iñ-kafartum Yawmañy-yaj-'alul-wildaana shiibaa–

18. 'As-samaaa-'u muñfaṭirum-bih? Kaana wa'-duhuu maf-'uulaa.

19. 'Inna haazihii Tazkirah: famañ shaaa-'attakhaza 'ilaa Rabbihii Sabiilaa! (Section 2)

---

16. But Pharaoh disobeyed the messenger; so We seized him with a heavy Punishment.

17. Then how shall ye, if ye deny (Allah), guard yourselves against a Day that will make children hoary-headed?—

18. Whereon the sky will be cleft asunder? His Promise needs must be accomplished.

19. Verily this is an Admonition: therefore, whoso will, let him take a (straight) path to his Lord !

20. 'Inna Rabbaka ya'-lamu 'annaka taquumu 'adnaa min-sulusayil-layli wa nisfahuu wa sulusahuu wa taaa-'ifatum-minallaziina ma-'ak. Wallaahu yuqaddirul-layla wan-nahaar. 'Alima 'allan-tuhsuuhu fataaba 'alay-kum faq-ra-'uu maa ta-yassara minal-Qur-'aan. 'Alima 'an-sayakuunu minkum-marzaa wa 'aakharuuna yazribuuna fil-'arzi yabtaguuna min-Fazlillaahi wa 'aakharuuna yuqaatiluuna fii Sabiilillaah. Faqra-'uu maa tayassara minhu wa 'aqiimus-Salaata wa 'aatuz-Zakaata wa 'aqrizul-laaha Qarzan Hasanaa. Wa maa tuqaddimuu li-'anfusikum-min khay-rin-tajiduuhu 'indal-laahi huwa khay-ranw-wa 'A'-zama 'Ajraa. Wastagfirul-laah: 'innallaaha Gafuurur-Rahiim.

---

20.   Thy Lord doth know that thou standest forth (to prayer) nigh two-thirds of the night, or half the night, or a third of the night, and so doth a party of those with thee. But Allah doth appoint Night and Day in due measure. He knoweth that ye are unable to keep count thereof. So He hath turned to you (in mercy): read ye, therefore, of the Qur'ān as much as may be easy for you. He knoweth that there may be (some) among you in ill-health; others travelling through the land, seeking of Allah's bounty; yet others fighting in Allah's Cause. Read ye, therefore, as much of the Qur'ān as may be easy (for you); and establish regular Prayer and give zakat; and loan to Allah a Beautiful Loan. And whatever good ye send forth for yourselves, ye shall find it with Allah. Yea, better and greater, in Reward, and seek ye the Grace of Allah: for Allah is Oft-Forgiving, Most Merciful.

Kahf–18
Verses 110–Sections 12

Bismillaahir-Rahmaanir-Rahiim.

1. 'Al-Hamdu lillaahil-laziii 'anzala 'alaa 'Abdihil-Kitaaba wa lam yaj-'al-lahuu 'iwajaa–

2. Qayyimal-li-yunzira Ba'-san-shadiidam-milladunhu wa yubash-shiral-Mu'-minii-nallaziina ya'-maluuna-s-saalihaati 'anna lahum 'Ajran hasanaa,

3. Maakisiina fiihi 'abadaa:

4. Wa yunzirallaziina qaalut-takhazallaahu waladaa:

5. Maa lahum-bihii min 'ilminwwa laa li-'aabaaa-'ihim. Kaburat kalimatan-takhruju min 'af-waahihim. 'Inyyaquuluuna 'illaa kazibaa.

Al-Kahf, or The Cave

In the name of Allah, Most Gracious, Most Merciful.

1. Praise be to Allah, Who hath sent to His Servant the Book, and hath allowed therein no Crookedness:

2. (He hath made it) Straight (and Clear) in order that He may warn (the godless) of a terrible Punishment from Him, and that He may give Glad Tidings to the Believers who work Righteous deeds, that they shall have a goodly Reward,

3. Wherein they shall remain for ever:

4. Further, that He may warn those (also) who say, "Allah hath begotten a son":

5. No knowledge have they of such a thing, nor had their fathers. It is a grievous thing that issues from their mouths as a saying. What they say is nothing but falsehood!

6. Fala-'allaka baakhi-'un-naf-
saka 'alaaa 'aasaarihim 'illam yu'-
minuu bi-haazal-Ḥadiisi 'asafaa.

7. 'Innaa ja'alnaa maa 'alal-'arẓi
ziinatal-lahaa linabluwa-hum 'ayyuhum 'aḥsanu 'ama-laa.

8. Wa 'innaa lajaa-'iluuna maa
'alayhaa ṣa'iidan-juruzaa.

9. 'Am hasibta 'anna 'Aṣ-ḥaa-
bal-Kahfi war-Raqiimi kaanuu min
'Aayaatinaa 'ajabaa?

10. 'Iz 'awal-fityatu 'ilal-Kahfi
faqaaluu Rabbanaaa 'aatinaa mil-
ladunka Raḥmataṅwwa hayyi' lanaa
min 'amrinaa rashadaa!

11. Faẓarabnaa 'alaaa 'aazaanihim fil-KAHFI siniina 'adadaa:

---

6. Thou wouldst only, perchance, Fret thyself to death, following after them, in grief, if they believe not in this Message.
7. That which is on earth We have made but as a glittering show for it, in order that We may test them—as to which of them are best in conduct.
8. Verily what is on earth We shall make but as dust and dry soil (without growth or herbage).
9. Or dost thou think that the Companions of the Cave and of the Inscription were wonders among Our Signs?
10. Behold, the youths betook themselves to the Cave: they said, "Our Lord! bestow on us mercy from Thyself, and dispose of our affair for us in the right way!"
11. Then We drew (a veil) over their ears, for a number of years, in the Cave, (so that they heard not):

12. Summa ba-'asnaahum li-na'-lama 'ayyul-ḥizbayni 'ah-saa limaa labiṣuuu 'amadaa! (Section 2)

13. Naḥnu naqussu 'alayka naba-'ahum-bil-Ḥaqq: 'inna-hum fityatun 'aamanuu bi-Rabbihim wa zidnaahum hudaa:

14. Wa rabaṭnaa 'alaa quluu-bihim 'iz qaamuu faqaaluu Rabbunaa Rabbus-samaawaati wal-'arẓi lan-nad-'uwa min duunihiii 'ilaahal-laqad qulnaaa 'izan-shatataa!

15. Haaa-'ulaaa-'i qawmunat-takhazuu min-duunihiii 'aalihah: Law laa ya'-tuuna 'alay-him-bi-sultaanim-bayyin? Fa-man 'aẓlamu mimma-niftaraa 'alallaahi kazibaa?

---

12. Then We roused them, in order to test which of the two parties was best at calculating the term of years they had tarried!

13. We relate to thee their story in truth: they were youths who believed in their Lord, and We increased them in guidance:

14. We gave strength to their hearts: behold, they stood up and said: "Our Lord is the Lord of the heavens and of the earth: never shall we call upon any god other than Him: if we did, we should indeed have uttered an enormity!

15. "These our people have taken for worship gods other than Him: why do they not bring forward an authority clear (and convincing) for what they do? Who doth more wrong than such as invent a falsehood against Allah?

16. Wa 'iẕi'-tazaltumuuhum wa maa ya'-buduuna 'illallaaha fa'-wuuu 'ilal-Kahfi yanshur lakum Rabbukum-mir-raḥma-tihii wa yuhayyi' lakum-min 'amrikum-mirfaqaa.

17. Wa tarash-shamsa 'izaa tala'at-tazaawaru 'an-Kahfihim ẕaatal-yamiini wa 'izaa gara-bat-taqri-ẕuhum ẕaatash-shi-maali wa hum fii fajwatim-minh. Ẕaalika min 'Aayaatil-laah: many-yahdillaahu fa-huwal-muhtad; wa many-yuẕ-lil falan- tajida lahuu waliyyam-murshidaa. (Section 3)

---

16. "When ye turn away from them and the things they worship other than Allah, betake yourselves to the Cave: your Lord will shower His mercies on you and dispose of your affair towards comfort and ease."

17. Thou wouldst have seen the sun, when it rose, declining to the right from their Cave, and when it set, turning away from them to the left, while they lay in the open space in the midst of the Cave. Such are among the Signs of Allah: he whom Allah guides is rightly guided; but he whom Allah leaves to stray,—for him wilt thou find no protector to lead him to the Right Way.

18. Wa taḥsabuhum 'ayqaa-ẓañwwa hum ruquud: wa nu-qallibuhum ẓaatal-yamiini wa ẓaatash-shimaal: wa kalbu-hum baasituñ-ziraa-'ayhi bil-wasiid: la-wiṭṭala'-ta 'alayhim la-wallayta minhum firaarañw- wa la-muli'-ta minhum ru'baa.

19. Wa kazaalika ba-'aṣnaa-hum li-yatasaaa-'aluu bayna-hum. Qaala qaaa-'ilum-min-hum kam labistum? Qaaluu labiṣnaa yawman 'aw ba'-ẕa yawm. Qaaluu Rabbukum 'a'-lamu bimaa labiṣtum...Fab-'aṣuuu 'ahadakum-biwa-riqikum haazihiii 'ilal-madii-nati fal-yañẓur 'ayyuhaaa 'az-kaa ta-'aaman-fal-ya'tikum-birizqim-minhu wal-yata-LAṬṬAF wa laa yush-'iranna bikum 'aḥadaa. (Half-Qur'ān)

---

18. Thou wouldst have thought them awake, whilst they were asleep, and We turned them on their right and on their left sides: their dog stretching forth his two fore-legs on the threshold: if thou hadst looked at them, thou wouldst have certainly turned back from them in flight, and wouldst certainly have been filled with terror of them.

19. Such (being their state), We raised them up (from sleep), that they might question each other. Said one of them, "How long have ye stayed (here)?" They said, "We have stayed (perhaps) a day, or part of a day." (At length) they (all) said, "Allah (alone) knows best how long ye have stayed here... Now send ye then one of you with this money of yours to the town: let him find out which is the best food (to be had) and bring some to you, (that ye may satisfy your hunger therewith) and let him behave with care and courtesy, and let him not inform anyone about you.

20. 'Innahum 'iny-yazharuu 'alaykum yarjumuukum 'aw yu-'iiduukum fii millatihim wa lan-tuflihuuu 'izan 'abadaa.

21. Wakazaalika 'a'-sarnaa 'alay-him liya'-lamuuu 'anna wa'-dallaahi haqqunwwa 'annas-Saa-'ata laa rayba fiihaa. 'Iz-yatanaaza-'uuna baynahum 'amrahum fa-qaalubnuu 'alay-him bunyaanaa: Rabbuhum 'a'-lamu bihim: qaalallaziina galabuu 'alaaa 'amrihim la-nat-takhizanna 'alayhim-masjidaa.

22. Sa-yaquuluuna salaasatur-raabi-'uhum kalbuhum: wa yaquuluuna khamsatun-saadisuhum kalbuhum rajmam-bil-gayb; wa yaquuluuna sab-'a-tunwwa saaminuhum kalbu-hum. Qur-Rabbiii 'a'-lamu bi'iddatihim-maa ya'-lamuhum 'illaa qaliil. Falaa tumaari fii-him 'illaa miraaa-'an-zaahiraa, wa laa tastafti fiihim-minhum 'ahadaa. (Section 4)

---

20. "For if they should come upon you, they would stone you or force you to return to their religion, and in that case ye would never attain prosperity."

21. Thus did We make their case know to the people, that they might know that the promise of Allah is true, and that there can be no doubt about the Hour of Judgement. Behold, they dispute among themselves as to their affair. (Some) said, "Construct a building over them": their Lord knows best about them: those who prevailed over their affair said, "Let us surely build a place of worship over them."

22. (Some) say they were three, the dog being the fourth among them; (others) say they were five, the dog being the sixth,—doubtfully guessing at the unknown; (yet others) say they were seven, the dog being the eighth. Say thou: "My Lord knoweth best their number; it is but few that know their (real case)." Enter not, therefore, into controversies concerning them, except on a matter that is clear, nor consult any of them about (the affair of) the Sleepers.

23.   Wa laa taquulanna lishay-'in 'innii faa-'ilun-zaalika gadaaa.

24.   'Illaaa 'any-yashaaa-'al-laah! Wazkur-Rabbaka 'izaa nasiita wa qul 'asaaa 'any-yah-diyani Rabbii li-'aqraba min haazaa rashadaa.

25.   Wa labisuu fii Kahfihim salaasa mi-'atin-siniina waz-daaduu tis-'aa.

26.   Qulillaahu 'a'-lamu bimaa labisuu: lahuu gaybus-samaa-waati wal-'arz: 'absir bihii wa 'asmi'! Maa lahum-min-duu-nihii minw-waliyy; wa laa yushriku fii Hukmihiii 'ahadaa.

27.   Watlu maaa 'uuhiya 'ilay-ka min-Kitaabi Rabbik: laa mubaddila li-Kalimaatih: wa lan-tajida min-duunihii multa-hadaa.

وَلَا تَقُوْلَنَّ لِشَائْءٍ اِنِّیْ فَاعِلٌ ذٰلِكَ غَدًا ۞ اِلَّا اَنْ يَّشَاءَ اللّٰهُ ۚ وَاذْكُرْ رَّبَّكَ اِذَا نَسِيْتَ وَقُلْ عَسٰى اَنْ يَّهْدِيَنِ رَبِّیْ لِاَقْرَبَ مِنْ هٰذَا رَشَدًا ۞

وَلَبِثُوْا فِیْ كَهْفِهِمْ ثَلٰثَ مِائَةٍ سِنِيْنَ وَازْدَادُوْا تِسْعًا ۞

قُلِ اللّٰهُ اَعْلَمُ بِمَا لَبِثُوْا ۚ لَهُ غَيْبُ السَّمٰوٰتِ وَالْاَرْضِ ؕ اَبْصِرْ بِهٖ وَاَسْمِعْ ؕ مَا لَهُمْ مِّنْ دُوْنِهٖ مِنْ وَّلِیٍّ ۖ وَّلَا يُشْرِكُ فِیْ حُكْمِهٖٓ اَحَدًا ۞

وَاتْلُ مَآ اُوْحِیَ اِلَيْكَ مِنْ كِتَابِ رَبِّكَ ۚ لَا مُبَدِّلَ لِكَلِمٰتِهٖ ۚ وَلَنْ تَجِدَ مِنْ دُوْنِهٖ مُلْتَحَدًا ۞

---

23.   Nor say of anything, "I shall be sure to do so and so tomorrow"—

24.   Except "If Allah so wills" and remember thy Lord when thou forgetnest, and say, "I hope that my Lord will guide me ever closer (even) than this to the right course."

25.   So they stayed in their Cave three hundred years, and nine (more).

26.   Say: "Allah knows best how long they stayed: with Him is (the knowledge of) the secrets of the heavens and the earth: how clearly He sees, how finely He hears (everything)! They have no protector other than Him; nor does He share His Command with any person whatsoever.

27.   And recite (and teach) what has been revealed to thee of the Book of thy Lord: none can change His Words, and none wilt thou find as a refuge other than Him.

28. Waṣbir nafsaka ma-'allaziina yad-'uuna Rabbahum-bil-gadaati wal-'ashiyyi yuriiduuna Waj-hahuu wa laa ta'-du 'aynaaka 'an-hum: turiidu ziinatal-Ḥayaa-tiddunyaa; wa laa tuti' man 'agfalnaa qalbahuu 'an-zikri-naa wattaba-'a hawaahu wa kaana 'amruhuu furutaa. (Part Three Fourth)

29. Wa qulil-Haqqu mir-Rabbi-kum: faman-shaaa-'a fal-yu'-miñ-wwa mañ-shaaa-'a fal-yak-fur: 'in-naaa 'a'-tadnaa liz-zaalimiina Naa-ran 'ahaata bi-him suraadiquhaa: wa 'iny-yastagiisuu yugaaṣuu bi-maaa-'iñ kalmuhli yashwil-wuj-uuh. Bi'-sash-sharaab! wa saaa-'at murtafaqaa!

30. 'Innallaziina 'aamanuu wa 'amiluṣ-ṣaalihaati 'innaa laa nuzii-'u 'ajra man 'ahsana 'amalaa.

---

28. And keep yourself content with those who call on their Lord morning and evening, seeking His Face; and let not thine eyes pass beyond them, seeking the pomp and glitter of this Life; nor obey any whose heart We have permitted to neglect the remembrance of Us, one who follows his own desires, and his affair has become all excess.

29. Say, "The Truth is from your Lord" let him who will, believe, and let him who will, reject (it): for the wrong-doers We have prepared a Fire whose (smoke and flames), like the walls and roof of a tent, will hem them in: if they implore relief they will be granted water like melted brass, that will scald their faces, how dreadful the drink! How uncomfor-table a couch to recline on!

30. As to those who believe and work righteousness, verily We shall not suffer to perish the reward of any who do a (single) righteous deed.

31. 'Ulaaa-'ika lahum Jannaatu 'Adnin tajrii min tahtihimul-'anhaaru yuhallawna fiihaa min 'asaawira min zahabinw-wa yalbasuuna siyaaban khuz-ram-min-sundusinwwa 'istab-raqim-muttaki-'iina fiihaa 'alal-'araaa-'ik. Ni'-mas-sa-waab! Wa hasunat murtafa-qaa! (Section 5)

أُولَـٰٓئِكَ لَهُمْ جَنَّـٰتُ عَدْنٍ تَجْرِى مِن تَحْتِهِمُ الْأَنْهَـٰرُ يُحَلَّوْنَ فِيهَا مِنْ أَسَاوِرَ مِن ذَهَبٍ وَّيَلْبَسُونَ ثِيَابًا خُضْرًا مِّن سُندُسٍ وَّإِسْتَبْرَقٍ مُّتَّكِئِينَ فِيهَا عَلَى الْأَرَآئِكِ نِعْمَ الثَّوَابُ وَحَسُنَتْ مُرْتَفَقًا ۝

32. Wazrib lahum-masalar-rajulayni ja-'alnaa li-'ahadihi-maa jannatayni min 'a'-naa-binwwa hafaf-naahumaa bi-nakhlinwwa ja-'alnaa bayna-humaa zar-'aa.

وَاضْرِبْ لَهُم مَّثَلًا رَّجُلَيْنِ جَعَلْنَا لِأَحَدِهِمَا جَنَّتَيْنِ مِنْ أَعْنَابٍ وَّحَفَفْنَـٰهُمَا بِنَخْلٍ وَّجَعَلْنَا بَيْنَهُمَا زَرْعًا ۝

33. Kiltal-jannatayni 'aatat 'ukulahaa wa lam tazlim-min-hu shay-'anw-wa fajjarnaa khi-laalahumaa naharaa,

كِلْتَا الْجَنَّتَيْنِ آتَتْ أُكُلَهَا وَلَمْ تَظْلِم مِّنْهُ شَيْئًا وَّفَجَّرْنَا خِلَـٰلَهُمَا نَهَرًا ۝

34. Wa kaana lahuu samar: faqaala li-saahibihii wa huwa yuhaawiruhuuu 'ana 'aksaru minka maalanwwa 'a-'azzu nafaraa.

وَكَانَ لَهُ ثَمَرٌ فَقَالَ لِصَاحِبِهِ وَهُوَ يُحَاوِرُهُ أَنَا أَكْثَرُ مِنكَ مَالًا وَّأَعَزُّ نَفَرًا ۝

---

31. For them will be Gardens of Eternity; beneath them rivers will flow: they will be adorned therein with bracelets of gold, and they will wear green garments of fine silk and heavy brocade; they will recline therein on raised thrones. How good the recompense! How beautiful a couch to recline on!

32. Set forth to them the parable of two men: For one of them We provided two gardens of grape-vines and surrounded them with date palms; in between the two We placed tillage.

33. Each of those gardens brought forth its produce, and failed not in the least therein: in the midst of them We caused a river to flow.

34. (Abundant) was the produce this man had: he said to his companion, in the course of a mutual argument: "More wealth have I than you, and more honour and power in (my following of) men."

35. Wa dakhala jannatahuu wa huwa zaalimul-li-nafsih: qaala maaa 'azunnu 'an-tabii-da haazihiii 'abadaa.

36. Wa maaa 'azunnus-Saa-'ata qaaa-'imatanwwa la-'irru-dittu 'ilaa Rabbii la-'ajidanna khayram-minhaa munqalabaa.

37. Qaala lahuu saahibuhuu wa huwa yu-haawiruhuuu 'aka-farta billazii khalaqaka min-turaabin-summa min-nutfatin-summa sawwaaka rajulaa?

38. Laakinna Huwallaahu Rabbii wa laaa 'ushriku bi-Rabbiii 'ahadaa.

39. Wa law laaa 'iz dakhalta jannataka qulta maa shaaa-'allaahu Laa quwwata 'illaa bil-laah! 'In-tarani 'ana 'aqalla minka maalanwwa waladaa.

---

35. He went into his garden while he wronged himself: he said, "I deem not that this will ever perish,"

36. "Nor do I deem that the Hour (of Judgement) will (ever) come: even if I am brought back to my Lord. I shall surely find (there) something better in exchange."

37. His companion said to him, in the course of the argument with him: "Dost thou deny Him Who created thee out of dust, then out of a sperm-drop, then fashioned thee into a man?

38. "But as for my part Allah is my Lord, and none shall I associate with my Lord.

39. "Why didst thou not, as thou wentest into Thy garden, say: 'Allah's Will (be done)! There is no power but from Allah!' If thou dost see me less than thee in wealth and sons,

40. Fa-'asaa Rabbiii 'any-yu'-tiyani khayram-min-jannatika wa yursila 'alayhaa husbaa-nam-minas-samaaa-'i fa-tusbi-ha sa-'iidan-zalaqaa!–

41. 'Aw yusbiha maaa-'uhaa gawran-falan-tastatii-'a lahuu talabaa.

42. Wa 'uhiita bi-samarihii fa-'as-baha yuqallibu kaffayhi 'alaa maaa 'anfaqa fiihaa wa hiya khaawiya-tun 'alaa 'uruushi-haa wa yaquulu yaa-laytanii lam 'ushrik bi-Rabbiii 'aha-daa!

43. Wa lam takul-lahuu fi-'a-tuny-yansuruunahuu min-duu-nillaahi wa maa kaana muntasiraa.

44. Hunaalikal-walaayatu lil-laahil-Haqq. Huwa Khayrun-sawaabanwwa Khayrun 'uqbaa. (Section 6)

---

40. "It may be that my Lord will give me something better than thy garden, and that He will send on thy garden thunderbolts (by way of reckoning) from heaven, making it (but) slippery sand!—

41. "Or the water of the garden will run off underground so that thou wilt never be able to find it."

42. So his fruits were encompassed (with ruin), and he remained twisting and turning his hands over what he had spent on his property, which had (now) tumbled to pieces to its very foundations, and he could only say, "Woe is me! Would I had never ascribed partners to my Lord and Cherisher!"

43. Nor had he numbers to help him against Allah, nor was he able to deliver himself.

44. There, the (only) protection comes from Allah, the True One. He is the Best to reward, and the Best to give success.

45. Waẕrib lahum-maṣalal-hayaatid-dunyaa kamaaa-'in 'añzalnaahu minas-samaaa-'i fakhtalata bihii nabaatul-'arẕi fa-'aṣbaha hashiiman-tazruuhur-riyaah: wa kaanal-laahu 'alaa kulli shay-'im-Muq-tadiraa.

46. 'Al-maalu wal-banuuna ziinatul-ḥayaatid-dunyaa: wal-baaqiyaatus-ṣaaliḥaatu khay-run 'iñda Rabbika ṣawaabañw-wa khayrun 'amalaa.

47. Wa yawma nusayyirul-ji-baala wa taral-'arẕa baariza-tañwwa hasharnaahum falam nugaadir minhum 'ahadaa.

48. Wa 'uriẕuu 'alaa Rabbika saffaa. Laqad ji'-tumuunaa ka-maa khalaqnaakum 'awwala marratim-bal-za-'amtum 'allan-naj-'ala lakum-maw-'idaa:

---

45. Set forth to them the similitude of the life of this world: it is like the rain which We send down from the skies: the earth's vegetation absorbs it, but soon it becomes dry stubble, which the winds do scatter: it is (only) Allah Who prevails over all things.

46. Wealth and sons are allurements of the life of this world: but the things that endure, Good Deeds, are best in the sight of thy Lord, as rewards, and best as (the foundation for) hopes.

47. On the Day We shall remove the mountains, and thou wilt see the earth as a level stretch, and We shall gather them, all together, nor shall We leave out anyone of them.

48. And they will be marshalled before thy Lord in ranks (with the announcement) , "Now have ye come to Us (bare) as We created you first: aye, ye thought We shall not fulfil the appointment made to you to meet (Us)!":

49. Wa wuẓi-'al-Kitaabu fa-taral-mujrimiina mushfiqiina mimmaa fiihi wa yuquuluuna yaa-waylatanaa maa li-haaẓal-kitaabi laa yu-gaadiru sagiira-tanwwa laa kabiiratan 'illaaa 'ahsaahaa! Wa wajaduu maa 'amiluu haaẓiraa: wa laa yaz-limu Rabbuka 'ahadaa. (Section 7)

50. Wa 'iz qulnaa lil-malaaa-'ikatis-juduu li-'Aadama fasa-jaduuu 'illaaa 'Ibliis. Kaana minal-Jinni fa-fasaqa 'an 'Am-ri Rabbih. 'Afa-tattakhiẓuu-nahuu wa ẓurriyyatahuuu 'aw-liyaaa-'a min-duunii wa hum lakum 'aduww! Bi'-sa liẓẓaa-limiina badalaa!

51. Maaa 'ash-hattuhum khal-qas-samaawaati wal-'arẓi wa laa khalqa 'anfusihim: wa maa kuntu muttakhiẓal-muẓilliina 'aẓudaa!

---

49. And the Book (of Deeds) will be placed (before you); and thou wilt see the sinful in great terror because of what is (recorded) therein; they will say, "Ah! woe to us! What a book is this! It leaves out nothing small or great, but takes account thereof!" They will find all that they did, placed before them: and not one will thy Lord treat with injustice.

50. Behold! We said to the angels, "Prostrate to Adam": they prostrated except Iblîs. He was one of the Jinns, and he broke the Command of his Lord will ye then take him and his progeny as protectors rather than Me? And they are enemies to you! Evil would be the exchange for the wrong-doers!

51. I called them not to witness the creation of the heavens and the earth, not (even) their own creation: nor is it for Me to take as helpers such as Lead (men) astray!

52.   Wa Yawma yaquulu naa-duu shurakaaa-'iyallaziina za-'amtum fada-'awhum falam yastajiibuu lahum wa ja-'alnaa baynahum-mawbiqaa.

53.   Wa ra-'al-mujrimuunan-Naara fa-zannuuu 'annahum-muwaaqi-'uuhaa wa lam yaji-duu 'anhaa masrifaa. (Section 8)

54.   Wa laqad sarrafnaa fii haa-zal-Qur-'aani linnaasi min-kulli masal: wa kaanal-'Insaanu 'aksara shay-'in-jadalaa.

55.   Wa maa mana-'annaasa 'any-yu'-minuuu 'iz jaaa-'a- humul-Hudaa wa yastagfiruu Rabbahum 'illaaa 'an-ta'-tiya-hum sunnatul-'awwaliina 'aw ya'-tiyahumul-'Azaabu qubu-laa?

---

52.   On the Day He will say, "Call on those whom ye thought to be My partners." And they will call on them, but they will not listen to them; and We shall make for them a place of common perdition.

53.   And the Sinful shall see the Fire and apprehend that they have to fall therein: no means will they find to turn away therefrom.

54.   We have explained in detail in this Qur'ān, for the benefit of mankind, every kind of similitude: but man is, in most things, contentious.

55.   And what is there to keep back men from believing, now that guidance has come to them, nor from praying for forgiveness from their Lord but that (they wait for) the ways of the ancients to overtake them, or the Wrath be brought to them face to face?

56. Wa maa nursilul-mursa-liina 'illaa mubash-shiriina wa muñziriin: wa yujaadilulla ziina kafaruu bil-baatili liyud-hizuu bihil-Haqqa wattakhazuuu 'Aayaatii wa maaa 'uñziruu huzuwaa!

وَمَا نُرْسِلُ الْمُرْسَلِيْنَ اِلَّا مُبَشِّرِيْنَ وَمُنْذِرِيْنَ ۚ وَيُجَادِلُ الَّذِيْنَ كَفَرُوْا بِالْبَاطِلِ لِيُدْحِضُوْا بِهِ الْحَقَّ وَاتَّخَذُوْٓا اٰيٰتِيْ وَمَآ اُنْذِرُوْا هُزُوًا ۞

57. Wa man 'azlamu mimmañ-zukkira bi-'Aayaati Rabbihii fa-'a'-raza 'anhaa wa nasiya maa qaddamat yadaah? 'Innaa ja-'alnaa 'alaa quluubihim 'akinnatan 'añyyafqahuuhu wa fii 'aazaanihim waqraa. Wa 'iñtad-'uhum 'ilal-Hudaa fa-lañy-yahtaduuu 'izan 'abadaa.

وَمَنْ اَظْلَمُ مِمَّنْ ذُكِّرَ بِاٰيٰتِ رَبِّهٖ فَاَعْرَضَ عَنْهَا وَنَسِيَ مَا قَدَّمَتْ يَدَاهُ ۚ اِنَّا جَعَلْنَا عَلٰى قُلُوْبِهِمْ اَكِنَّةً اَنْ يَّفْقَهُوْهُ وَفِيْٓ اٰذَانِهِمْ وَقْرًا ۚ وَاِنْ تَدْعُهُمْ اِلَى الْهُدٰى فَلَنْ يَّهْتَدُوْٓا اِذًا اَبَدًا ۞

58. Wa Rabbukal-Gafuuru Zur-Rahmah. Law yu-'aakhi-zuhum-bimaa kasabuu la-'aj-jala lahumul-'azaab: bal-la-hum-maw-'idul-lañy-yajiduu miñ-duunihii maw-'ilaa.

وَرَبُّكَ الْغَفُوْرُ ذُو الرَّحْمَةِ ۚ لَوْ يُؤَاخِذُهُمْ بِمَا كَسَبُوْا لَعَجَّلَ لَهُمُ الْعَذَابَ ۚ بَلْ لَّهُمْ مَّوْعِدٌ لَّنْ يَّجِدُوْا مِنْ دُوْنِهٖ مَوْئِلًا ۞

---

56. We only send the Messengers to give glad tidings and to give warnings: but the Unbelievers dispute with vain argument, in order therewith to weaken the truth, and they treat My Signs and warnings as a jest.

57. And who doth more wrong than one who is reminded of the Signs of his Lord but turns away from them, forgetting the (deeds) which his hands have sent forth? Verily We have set veils over their hearts so that they understand this not, and over their ears, deafness. If thou callest them to guidance, even then will they never accept guidance.

58. But your Lord is Most Forgiving, full of Mercy. If He were to call them (at once) to account for what they have earned, then surely He would have hastened their Punishment: but they have their appointed time, beyond which they will find no refuge.

59. Wa tilkal-quraaa 'ahlak-naahum lammaa zalamuu wa ja-'alnaa li-mahlikihim-maw-'idaa. (Section 9)

60. Wa 'iz qaala Muusaa li-fataahu laaa 'abrahu hattaaa 'abluga majma-'al-bahrayni 'aw 'amziya huqubaa.

61. Falammaa balagaa maj-ma-'a baynihimaa nasiyaa huutahumaa fattakhaza sabiilahuu fil-bahri sarabaa.

62. Falammaa jaawazaa qaala li-fataahu 'aatinaa gadaaa-'a-naa laqad laqiinaa min-safa-rinaa haazaa nasabaa.

63. Qaala 'ara-'ayta 'iz 'away-naaa 'ilas-sakhrati fa-'innii nasiitul-huut? wa maaa 'ansaanii-hu 'illash-Shaytaanu 'an 'az-kurah: wattakhaza sabiilahuu fil-bahri 'ajabaa!

64. Qaala zaalika maa kunnaa nabgi fartaddaa 'alaaa 'aa-saari-himaa qasasaa.

---

59. Such were the towns We destroyed when they committed iniquities; but We fixed an appointed time for their destruction.

60. Behold, Moses said to his attendant, "I will not give up until I reach the junction of the two seas or (until) I spend years and years in travel."

61. But when they reached the Junction, they forgot (about) their Fish, which took its course through the sea (straight) as in a tunnel.

62. When they had passed on (some distance), Moses said to his attendant: "Bring us our early meal; truly we have suffered much fatigue at this (stage of) our journey."

63. He replied: "Sawest thou (what happened) when we betook ourselves to the rock? I did indeed forget (about) the Fish: none but Satan made me forget to tell (you) about It: it took its course through the sea in a marvellous way!"

64. Moses said: "That was what we were seeking after: so they went back on their footsteps, following (the path they had come).

65. Fa-wajadaa 'Abdam-min 'ibaadinaaa 'aataynaahu Raḥ-matam-min 'iṅdinaa wa 'allam-naahu mil-Ladunnaa 'Ilmaa.

فَوَجَدَا عَبْدًا مِّنْ عِبَادِنَا آتَيْنَاهُ رَحْمَةً مِّنْ عِنْدِنَا وَعَلَّمْنَاهُ مِنْ لَّدُنَّا عِلْمًا ۝

66. Qaala lahuu Muusaa hal-'attabi-'uka 'alaaa 'aṅ-tu-'alli-mani mimmaa 'ullimta rush-daa?

قَالَ لَهُ مُوسَى هَلْ أَتَّبِعُكَ عَلَى أَنْ تُعَلِّمَنِ مِمَّا عُلِّمْتَ رُشْدًا ۝

67. Qaala 'innaka laṅ-tasta-ṭii-'a ma-'iya sabraa!

قَالَ إِنَّكَ لَنْ تَسْتَطِيعَ مَعِيَ صَبْرًا ۝

68. Wa kayfa taṣbiru 'alaa maa lam tuḥiṭ bihii khubraa?

وَكَيْفَ تَصْبِرُ عَلَى مَا لَمْ تُحِطْ بِهِ خُبْرًا ۝

69. Qaala satajiduniii 'iṅ-shaaa-'allaahu saabiranwwa laaa 'a'-ṣii laka 'amraa.

قَالَ سَتَجِدُنِي إِنْ شَاءَ اللهُ صَابِرًا وَّلَا أَعْصِي لَكَ أَمْرًا ۝

70. Qaala fa-'inittaba'-tanii falaa tas-'annii 'aṅ shay-'in hattaaa 'uḥdiṣa laka minhu ẕikraa (Section 10)

قَالَ فَإِنِ اتَّبَعْتَنِي فَلَا تَسْئَلْنِي عَنْ شَيْءٍ حَتَّى أُحْدِثَ لَكَ مِنْهُ ذِكْرًا ۝

71. Faṅtalaqaa: hattaaa 'izaa rakibaa fis-safiinati kharaqahaa. Qaala 'a-kharaqtahaa li-tugri-qa 'ahlahaa? Laqad ji'-ta shay-'an 'imraa!

فَانْطَلَقَا حَتَّى إِذَا رَكِبَا فِي السَّفِينَةِ خَرَقَهَا قَالَ أَخَرَقْتَهَا لِتُغْرِقَ أَهْلَهَا لَقَدْ جِئْتَ شَيْئًا إِمْرًا ۝

---

65. So they found one of Our servants. On whom We had bestowed Mercy from Ourselves and whom We had taught knowledge from Our own presence.

66. Moses said to him: "May I follow thee, on the footing that Thou teach me something of the (Higher) Truth which thou hast been taught?"

67. (The other) said: "Verily Thou wilt not be able to have patience with me!

68. "For how canst thou have patience about things which are beyond your knowledge?"

69. Moses said: "Thou wilt find me, if Allah so will, (truly) patient: nor shall I disobey thee in aught."

70. The other said: "If then thou wouldst follow me, ask me no questions about anything until I Myself speak to thee concerning it."

71. So they both proceeded: until, when they were in the boat, he scuttled it. Said Moses: "Hast thou scuttled it in order to drown those in it? Truly a strange thing hast thou done!"

72. Qaala 'alam 'aqul 'innaka lañ-tastaṭii-'a ma-'iya   sabraa?

قَالَ اَلَمۡ اَقُلۡ اِنَّكَ لَنۡ تَسۡتَطِيۡعَ مَعِیَ صَبۡرًا ۞

73. Qaala laa tu-'aakhiẓnii b i m a a n a s i i t u wa laa turhiqnii min 'amrii 'usraa.

قَالَ لَا تُؤَاخِذۡنِیۡ بِمَا نَسِيۡتُ وَلَا تُرۡهِقۡنِیۡ مِنۡ اَمۡرِیۡ عُسۡرًا ۞

74. Fañtalaqaa: hattaaa 'izaa laqiyaa gulaamañ-faqatalahuu qaala 'aqatalta nafsañ-zakiy-yatam-bi-gayri nafs? Laqad ji'-ta shay-'an-nukraa!

فَانۡطَلَقَا فَحَتّٰى اِذَا لَقِيَا غُلٰمًا فَقَتَلَهٗ قَالَ اَقَتَلۡتَ نَفۡسًا زَكِيَّةَ بِغَيۡرِ نَفۡسٍ لَقَدۡ جِئۡتَ شَيۡئًا نُّكۡرًا ۞

75. **QAALA 'ALAM** 'aqul-laka 'innaka lañ-tastatii-'a ma-'iya sabraa?

قَالَ اَلَمۡ اَقُلۡ لَّكَ اِنَّكَ لَنۡ تَسۡتَطِيۡعَ مَعِیَ صَبۡرًا ۞

76. Qaala 'iñ-sa-'altuka 'añ-shay-'im-ba'-dahaa falaa tu-ṣaaḥibnii: qad balagta milla-dunnii 'uẓraa.

قَالَ اِنۡ سَاَلۡتُكَ عَنۡ شَیۡءٍ بَعۡدَهَا فَلَا تُصٰحِبۡنِیۡ قَدۡ بَلَغۡتَ مِنۡ لَّدُنِّیۡ عُذۡرًا ۞

---

72. He answered: "Did I not tell thee that thou canst have no patience with me?"

73. Moses said: Rebuke me not for forgetting, nor grieve me by raising difficulties in my case."

74. Then they proceeded: until, when they met a young boy, he slew him. Moses said: "Hast thou slain an innocent person who had slain none? Truly a foul (unheard-of) thing hast thou done!"

75. He answered: "Did I not tell thee that thou canst have no patience with me?"

76. (Moses) said: "If ever I ask thee about anything after this, keep me not in thy company: then wouldst thou have received (full) excuse from my side.

77. Fanṭalaqaa: Ḥattaaa ’izaaa ’atayaaa ’ahla-qaryati-nistat‘a-maaa ’ahlahaa fa-’abaw ’añy-yuẓayyifuuhumaa fa-wajadaa fiihaa jidaarañy-yuriidu ’any-yañqaẓẓa fa-’aqaamah. Qaala law shi’-ta lattakhaẓta ‘alayhi ’ajraa.

78. Qaala haaẓaa firaaqu bay-nii wa baynik: sa-’unabbi-’uka bi-ta’-wiili maa lam tastaṭi‘-‘alayhi ṣabraa.

79. ’Ammas-safiinatu fakaa-nat li-masaakiina ya‘-maluuna fil-baḥri fa-’arattu ’an ’a-‘iiba-haa wa kaana waraaa-’ahum-malikuñy-ya’khuẓu kulla safii-natin gaṣbaa.

80. Wa ’ammal-gulaamu fa-kaana ’abawaahu Mu’-minay-ni fa-khashi-inaaa ’añy-yurhi-qahumaa ṭug-yaananwwa kuf-raa.

---

77. Then they proceeded: until, when they came to the inhabitants of a town, they asked them for food, but they refused them hospitality. They found there a wall on the point of falling down, but he set it up straight. (Moses) said: "If thou hadst wished, surely thou couldst have exacted some recompense for it!

78. He answered: "This is the parting between me and thee: now will I tell thee the interpretation of (those things) over which thou wast unable to hold patience.

79. "As for the boat, it belonged to certain men in dire want: they plied on the water: I but wished to render it unserviceable, for there was after them a certain king who seized on every boat by force.

80. "As for the youth, his parents were people of Faith, and we feared that he would grieve them by obstinate rebellion and ingratitude (to Allah)

81. Fa-'aradnaaa 'any-yubdila-humaa Rabbuhumaa khayram-minhu zakaatanwwa 'aqraba ruhmaa.

82. Wa 'ammal-jidaaru fakaa-na li-gulaamayni yatiimayni fil-Madi-inati wa kaana tahta-huu kanzul-lahumaa wa kaana 'abuuhumaa saali-haa: fa-'araada Rabbuka 'any-yab-lugaaa 'ashuddahumaa wa yasta-khrijaa kanzahumaa rahmatam-mir-Rabbik. Wa maa fa-'altuhuu 'an 'amrii. Zaalika ta'-wiilu maa lam-tas-ti' 'alayhi sabraa. (Section 11)

83. Wa yas-'aluunaka 'an-Zil-Qarnayn. Qul sa-'atluu 'alay-kum-minhu zikraa.

84. 'Innaa makkannaa lahuu fil-'arzi wa 'aataynaahu min kulli shay-'in-sababaa.

85. Fa-'atba-'a sababaa,

---

81. "So we desired that their Lord would give them in exchange (a son) better in purity (of conduct) and closer in affection.

82. "As for the wall, it belonged to two youths, orphans, in the Town; there was, beneath it; a buried treasure, to which they were entitled; their father had been a righteous man: so thy Lord desired that they should attain their age of full strength and get out their treasure—a mercy (and favour) from thy Lord. I did it not of my own accord. Such is the interpretation of (those things) over which thou wast unable to hold patience."

83. They ask thee concerning *Zulqarnain.* Say, "I will rehearse to you something of his story."

84. Verily We established his power on earth, and We gave him the ways and the means to all ends.

85. One (such) way he followed,

86. Ḥattaaa 'izaa balaga magri-bashshamsi wajadahaa tagrubu fii 'aynin hami-'atiñwwa waja-da 'iñdahaa Qawmaa. Qulnaa yaa-Zal-Qarnayni 'immaaa 'an tu-'azziba wa 'immaaa 'an tat-takhiza fiihim ḥusnaa

87. Qaala 'ammaa mañ zalama fa-sawfa nu-'azzibuhuu summa yurad-du 'ilaa Rabbihii fayu-'azzibuhuu 'azaaban-nukraa.

88. Wa 'ammaa man 'aamana wa 'amila saaliḥañ-falahuu ja-zaaa-'anil-ḥusnaa, wa sana-quulu lahuu min 'amrinaa yusraa.

89. Summa 'atba'a sababaa.

90. Ḥattaaa 'izaa balaga mat-li-'ash-shamsi wajadahaa tat-lu-'u 'alaa qawmil-lam-naj-'al-lahum-miñ-duunihaa sitraa

91. Kazaalik: wa qad 'aḥat-naa bimaa ladayhi khubraa.

92. Summa 'atba-'a sababaa,

---

86.   Until, when he reached the setting of the sun, he found it set in a spring of murky water: near it he found a People: We said: "O Zul-qarnain! (thou hast authority,) either to punish them, or to treat them with kindness."

87.   He said: "Whoever doth wrong, him shall we punish; then shall he be sent back to his Lord; and He will punish him with a punishment unheard-of (before).

88.   "But whoever believes, and works righteousness,—he shall have a goodly reward, and easy will be his task as we order it by our command."

89.   Then followed he (another) way,

90.   Until, when he came to the rising of the sun, he found it rising on a people for whom We had provided no covering protection against the sun.

91.   (He left them) as they were: We completely understood what was before him.

92.   Then followed he (another) way,

93. Ḥattaaa 'iẓaa balaga bay-nas-saddayni wajada min-duu-nihimaa qawmal-laa yakaa-duuna yafqahuuna qawlaa,

حَتّٰى إِذَا بَلَغَ بَيْنَ السَّدَّيْنِ وَجَدَ مِنْ دُوْنِهِمَا قَوْمًا لَّا يَكَادُوْنَ يَفْقَهُوْنَ قَوْلًا ۝

94. Qaaluu yaa-Zal-Qarnayni 'inna Ya'-juuja wa Ma'-juuja mufsiduuna fil-'arẓi fahal naj-'alu laka kharjan 'alaaa 'an-taj'ala baynanaa wa baynahum sad-daa?

قَالُوْا يَاذَا الْقَرْنَيْنِ إِنَّ يَأْجُوْجَ وَمَأْجُوْجَ مُفْسِدُوْنَ فِى الْأَرْضِ فَهَلْ نَجْعَلُ لَكَ خَرْجًا عَلٰى أَنْ تَجْعَلَ بَيْنَنَا وَبَيْنَهُمْ سَدًّا ۝

95. Qaala maa makkannii fiihi Rabbii khayrun-fa-'a- 'iinuunii bi-quwwatin 'aj-'al baynakum wa baynahum radmaa:

قَالَ مَا مَكَّنِّىْ فِيْهِ رَبِّىْ خَيْرٌ فَأَعِيْنُوْنِىْ بِقُوَّةٍ أَجْعَلْ بَيْنَكُمْ وَبَيْنَهُمْ رَدْمًا ۝

96. 'Aatuunii zubaral-hadiid. Ḥattaaa 'iẓaa saawaa baynas-sadafayni qaalanfukhuu: hat-taaa 'iẓaa ja-'alahuu naaran qaala 'aatuuniii 'ufrig 'alayhi qiṭraa.

اٰتُوْنِىْ زُبَرَ الْحَدِيْدِ حَتّٰى إِذَا سَاوٰى بَيْنَ الصَّدَفَيْنِ قَالَ انْفُخُوْا حَتّٰى إِذَا جَعَلَهُ نَارًا قَالَ اٰتُوْنِىْ أُفْرِغْ عَلَيْهِ قِطْرًا ۝

---

93. Until, when he reached (a tract) between two mountains, he found, beneath them, a people who scarcely understood a word.

94. They said: "O Zulqarnain! the Gog and Magog (people) do great mischief on earth: shall we then render thee tribute in order that thou mightest erect a barrier between us and them?

95. He said: "(The power) in which my Lord has established me is better (than tribute): help me therefore with strength (and labour): I will erect a strong barrier between you and them:

96. "Bring me blocks of iron." At length, when he had filled up the space between the two steep mountain-sides, he said, "Blow (with your bellows)" then, when he had made it (red) as fire, he said: "Bring me, that I may pour over it, molten lead."

97. Famastaa-'uuu 'any-yaz-haruuhu wa mastataa-'uu la-huu naqbaa.

98. Qaala haazaa rahmatum-mir-Rabbii: fa-'izaa jaaa-'a wa'-du Rabbii ja-'alahuu dak-kaaa'; wa kaana wa'-du Rabbii haqqaa.

99. Wa taraknaa ba'-zahum Yawma-'iziny-yamuuju fii ba'-zinwwa nufikha fiṣ-Ṣuuri fa-jama'-naahum jam-'aa.

100. Wa 'araznaa Jahannama Yawma-'izil-lil-kaafiriina 'ar-zaa,—

101. 'Allaziina kaanat 'a'-yu-nuhum fii gitaaa-'in 'an zikrii wa kaanuu laa yastatii-'uuna sam-'aa. (Section 12)

---

97. Thus were they made powerless to scale it or to dig through it.

98. He said: "This is a mercy from my Lord: but when the promise of my Lord comes to pass, He will make it into dust; and the promise of my Lord is true."

99. On that day We shall leave them to surge like waves on one another: the trumpet will be blown, and We shall collect them all together.

100. And We shall present Hell that day for Unbelievers to see, all spread out,—

101. (Unbelievers) whose eyes had been under a veil from Remembrance of Me, and who had been unable even to hear.

102. 'Afahasi-ballaziina kafaruuu 'any-yattakhizuu 'ibaadii min-duuniii 'awliyaaa'? 'In-naaa 'a'-tadnaa Jahannama lil-kaafiriina nuzulaa.

103. Qul hal nunabbi-'ukum-bil-'akhsariina 'a'-maalaa?

104. 'Allaziina zalla sa'-yuhum fil-hayaatiddunyaa wa hum yah-sabuuna 'annahum yuhsinuuna sun-'aa?

105. 'Ulaaa-'ikallaziina kafaruu bi-'Aayaati Rabbihim wa Liqaaa-'ihii fa-habitat 'a'-maa-luhum falaa nuqiimu lahum Yawmal-Qiyaamati waznaa.

106. Zaalika jazaaa-'uhum Jahannamu bimaa kafaruu watta-khazuuu 'Aayaatii wa Rusulii huzuwaa.

107. 'Innallaziina 'aamanuu wa 'amilus-saalihaati kaanat lahum Jannaatul-Firdawsi nu-zulaa,

---

102. Do the Unbelievers think that they can take My servants as protectors besides Me? Verily We have prepared Hell for the Unbelievers for (their) entertainment.

103. Say: "Shall we tell you of those who lose most in respect of their deeds?—

104. "Those whose efforts have been wasted in this life, while they thought that they were acquiring good by their works?"

105. They are those who deny the Signs of their Lord and the fact of their having to meet Him (in the Hereafter): vain will be their works, nor shall We, on the Day of Judgment, give them any Weight.

106. That is their reward, Hell; because they rejected Faith, and took My Signs and My Messengers by way of jest.

107. As to those who believe and work righteous deeds, they have, for their entertainment, the Gardens of Paradise,

108. Khaalidiina fiihaa laa yabguuna 'anhaa ḥiwalaa.

خٰلِدِيْنَ فِيْهَا لَا يَبْغُوْنَ عَنْهَا حِوَلًا ۝

109. Qul-law kaanal-bahru midaadal-li-Kalimaati Rabbii lanafidal-bahru qabla 'an-tan-fada Kalimaatu Rabbii wa law ji'-naa bi-miṣlihii madadaa.

قُلْ لَّوْ كَانَ الْبَحْرُ مِدَادًا لِّكَلِمٰتِ رَبِّيْ لَنَفِدَ الْبَحْرُ قَبْلَ اَنْ تَنْفَدَ كَلِمٰتُ رَبِّيْ وَلَوْ جِئْنَا بِمِثْلِهٖ مَدَدًا ۝

110. Qul 'innamaaa 'ana basharum-miṣlukum yuuhaaa 'ilayya 'annamaaa 'Ilaahukum 'Ilaahunw-Waahid: faman kaana yarjuu Liqaaa-'a Rabbihii fal-ya'-mal 'amalan ṣaaliḥanwwa laa yushrik bi-'ibaadati Rabbihiii 'ahadaa.

قُلْ اِنَّمَا اَنَا بَشَرٌ مِّثْلُكُمْ يُوْحٰى اِلَيَّ اَنَّمَا اِلٰهُكُمْ اِلٰهٌ وَّاحِدٌ ۚ فَمَنْ كَانَ يَرْجُوْا لِقَاءَ رَبِّهٖ فَلْيَعْمَلْ عَمَلًا صَالِحًا وَّلَا يُشْرِكْ بِعِبَادَةِ رَبِّهٖ اَحَدًا ۝

---

108. Wherein they shall dwell (for aye): no change will they wish for from them.

109. Say: "If the ocean were ink (wherewith to write out) the words of my Lord, sooner would the ocean be exhausted than would the words of my Lord, even if we added another ocean like it, for its aid."

110. Say: "I am but a man like yourselves, (but) the inspiration has come to me, that your God is One God: whoever expects to meet his Lord, let him work righteousness, and, in the worship of his Lord, admit no one as partner.

Maryam–19
Verses 98–Sections 6

Bismillaahir-Raḥmaanir-Raḥiim.
1. Kaaaf-Haa-Yaa-'Ayyyn̄-Saaad.
2. Ẕikru Rahmati Rabbika 'abdahuu Zakariyyaa.

3. 'Iz naaḍaa Rabbahuu ni-ḍaaa-'an khafiyyaa.

4. Qaala Rabbi 'innii wahanal-'aẓmu minnii washta-'alar-ra'-su shaybañwwa lam 'akum-bi-du-'aaa-'ika Rabbi shaqiyyaa!

5. Wa 'innii khiftul-mawaa liya miñwwaraaa-'ii wa kaana-timra-'atii 'aaqirañ-fahab lii milladuñka waliyyaa,–

6. Yariṣunii wa yarisu min 'aali Ya'-quuba waj-'alhu Rabbi raẓiyyaa!

Maryam, or Mary

In the name of Allah, Most Gracious, Most Merciful.
1. Kãf. Hã. Yã. 'Ain. Sãd.
2. (This is) a mention of the Mercy of thy Lord to His servant Zakarîya.
3. Behold! he cried to his Lord in secret.
4. Praying: "O my Lord! infirm indeed are my bones, and the hair of my head doth glisten with grey: but never am I unblest, O my Lord, in my prayer to Thee!
5. "Now I fear (what) my relatives (and colleagues) (will do) after me: but my wife is barren: so give me an heir as from Thyself,—
6. "(One that) will (truly) inherit me, and inherit the posterity of Jacob; and make him, O my Lord! One with whom Thou art well-pleased!"

7. Yaa-Zakariyyaaa 'innaa nubashshiruka bi-gulaami-nismu-huu Yahyaa lam naj-'al-lahuu miñ-qablu samiyyaa.

8. Qaala Rabbi 'annaa yakuu-nu lii gulaamuñwwa kaanatim-ra-'atii 'aaqiranwwa qad ba-lagtu minal-kibari 'itiyyaa?

9. Qaala kazaalik: qaala Rabbuka huwa 'alayya hay- yinuñwwa qad khalaqtuka miñ-qablu wa lam taku shay-'aa!

10. Qaala Rabbij-'al-liii 'Aayah. Qaala 'Aayatuka 'allaa tukallimannaasa salaaṣa la-yaalin-sa-wiyyaa.

11. Fa-kharaja 'alaa qawmi-hii minal-mihraabi fa-'awhaaa 'ilayhim 'añ sabbiḥuu bukra-tanwwa 'ashiyyaa.

12. Yaa-Yahyaa khuzil- Kitaaba bi-quwwwah: wa 'aataynaahul-Ḥukma ṣabiyyaa.

---

7. (His prayer was answered): "O Zakarîya! We give thee good news of a son: his name shall be Yahya: on none by that name have We conferred distinction before."

8. He said: "O my Lord! how shall I have a son, when my wife is barren and I have grown quite decrepit from old age?"

9. He said: "So (it will be): thy Lord saith, 'That is easy for Me: I did indeed create thee before, when thou hadst been nothing!'"

10. (Zakarîya) said: "O my Lord! give me a Sign," "Thy Sign," was the answer, "Shall be that thou shalt speak to no man for three nights, although thou art not dumb."

11. So Zakarîya came out to his people from his chamber: he told them by signs to celebrate Allah's praises in the morning and in the evening.

12. (To his son came the command): "O Yahyā! take hold of the Book with might": and We gave him Wisdom even as a youth,

13. Wa ḥanaanam-milladun-naa wa zakaah: wa kaana ta-qiyyaa,

وَحَنَانًا مِّنْ لَّدُنَّا وَزَكَوةً ۖ وَكَانَ تَقِيًّا ۞

14. Wa barram-bi-waalidayhi wa lam yakuṇ jabbaaran ‘asiyyaa.

وَبَرًّا بِوَالِدَيْهِ وَلَمْ يَكُنْ جَبَّارًا عَصِيًّا

15. Wa Salaamun ‘alayhi yaw-ma wulida wa yawma yamuutu wa yawma yub-‘aṣu ḥayyaa! (Section 2)

وَسَلَامٌ عَلَيْهِ يَوْمَ وُلِدَ وَيَوْمَ يَمُوتُ وَيَوْمَ يُبْعَثُ حَيًّا ۞

16. Wazkur fil-Kitaabi Mar-yam. ’Iziṇtabaẓat min ’ahlihaa makaanaṇ-sharqiyyaa.

وَاذْكُرْ فِي الْكِتَابِ مَرْيَمَ ۚ إِذِ انتَبَذَتْ مِنْ أَهْلِهَا مَكَانًا شَرْقِيًّا ۞

17. Fattakhaẓat miṇ duunihim hijaabaa. Fa-’arsalnaaa ’ilay-haa ruuhanaa fa-tamassala lahaa basharaṇ-sawiyyaa.

فَاتَّخَذَتْ مِن دُونِهِمْ حِجَابًا فَأَرْسَلْنَا إِلَيْهَا رُوحَنَا فَتَمَثَّلَ لَهَا بَشَرًا سَوِيًّا ۞

18. Qaalat ’inniii ’a-‘uuzu bir-Rahmaani miṇka ’iṇ-kuṇta taqiyyaa.

قَالَتْ إِنِّي أَعُوذُ بِالرَّحْمَٰنِ مِنكَ إِن كُنتَ تَقِيًّا ۞

19. Qaala ’innamaaa ana rasuulu Rabbiki li-’ahaba laki gulaamaṇ-zakiyyaa.

قَالَ إِنَّمَا أَنَا رَسُولُ رَبِّكِ لِأَهَبَ لَكِ غُلَامًا زَكِيًّا ۞

---

13. And pity (for all creatures) as from Us, and purity: he was devout,
14. And kind to his parents, and he was not overbearing or rebellious.
15. So Peace on him the day he was born, the day that he dies, and the day that he will be raised up to life (again)!
16. Relate in the Book (the story of) Mary, when she withdrew from her family to a place in the East.
17. She placed a screen (to screen herself) from them: then We sent to her Our angel, and he appeared before her as a man in all respects.
18. She said: "I seek refuge from thee to (Allah) Most Gracious: (come not near) if thou dost fear Allah."
19. He said: "Nay, I am only a messenger from thy Lord (to announce) to thee the gift of a pure son."

20. Qaalat 'annaa yakuunu lii gulaamuñwwa lam yamsasnii basharuñwwa lam 'aku bagiy-yaa? (Part One-fourth)

قَالَتْ اَنّٰى يَكُوْنُ لِيْ غُلٰمٌ وَّلَمْ يَمْسَسْنِيْ بَشَرٌ وَّلَمْ اَكُ بَغِيًّا ۝

21. Qaala kazaalik: qaala Rabbuki huwa 'alayya hayyin: wa linaj-'alahuuu 'Aayatal-linnaasi wa Rahmatam-min-naa: wa kaana 'amram-maq-ziyyaa.

قَالَ كَذٰلِكِ ۚ قَالَ رَبُّكِ هُوَ عَلَيَّ هَيِّنٌ ۚ وَلِنَجْعَلَهٗ اٰيَةً لِّلنَّاسِ وَرَحْمَةً مِّنَّا ۚ وَكَانَ اَمْرًا مَّقْضِيًّا ۝

22. Fa-hamalat-hu fañtabazat bihii makaanañ-qasiyyaa.

فَحَمَلَتْهُ فَانْتَبَذَتْ بِهٖ مَكَانًا قَصِيًّا ۝

23. Fa-'ajaaa-'ahal-makhaazu 'ilaa jiz-'innakhlah; qaalat yaa-laytanii mittu qabla haa-zaa wa kuntu nasyam-mañ-siyyaa!

فَاَجَاءَهَا الْمَخَاضُ اِلٰى جِذْعِ النَّخْلَةِ ۚ قَالَتْ يٰلَيْتَنِيْ مِتُّ قَبْلَ هٰذَا وَكُنْتُ نَسْيًا مَّنْسِيًّا ۝

24. Fa-naadaahaa miñ-tahti-haaa 'allaa tahzanii qad ja-'ala Rabbuki tahtaki sariyyaa;

فَنَادَاهَا مِنْ تَحْتِهَا اَلَّا تَحْزَنِيْ قَدْ جَعَلَ رَبُّكِ تَحْتَكِ سَرِيًّا ۝

25. Wa huzziii 'ilayki bijiz-'in-nakhlati tusaaqit 'alayki ruta-bañ-janiyyaa.

وَهُزِّيْ اِلَيْكِ بِجِذْعِ النَّخْلَةِ تُسٰقِطْ عَلَيْكِ رُطَبًا جَنِيًّا ۝

---

20. She said: "How shall I have a son, seeing that no man has touched me, and I am not unchaste?"

21. He said: "So (it will be): thy Lord saith, 'That is easy for Me: and (We wish) to appoint him as a Sign unto men and a Mercy from Us': it is a matter (so) decreed."

22. So she conceived him, and she retired with him to a remote place.

23. And the pains of childbirth drove her to the trunk of a palm-tree: she cried (in her anguish): "Ah! would that I had died before this! would that I had been a thing forgotten.

24. But (a voice) cried to her from beneath the (palm-tree): "Grieve not! for thy Lord hath provided a rivulet beneath thee;

25. "And shake towards thyself the trunk of the palm-tree: it will let fall fresh ripe dates upon thee.

26. Fa-kulii washrabii wa qar-rii 'aynaa. Fa-'immaa tara-yinna minal-bashari 'aḥadan fa-quuliii 'innii naẓartu lir-Rahmaani ṣawmañ-falan 'ukal-limal-yawma 'iñsiyyaa.

فَكُلِى وَاشْرَبِى وَقَرِّى عَيْنًا ۚ فَاِمَّا تَرَيِنَّ مِنَ الْبَشَرِ اَحَدًا ۙ فَقُوْلِىٓ اِنِّى نَذَرْتُ لِلرَّحْمٰنِ صَوْمًا فَلَنْ اُكَلِّمَ الْيَوْمَ اِنْسِيًّا ۞

27. Fa-'atat bihii qawmahaa tahmiluh. Qaaluu yaa-Marya-mu laqad ji'-ti shay-'añ-fariy-yaa.

فَاَتَتْ بِهٖ قَوْمَهَا تَحْمِلُهٗ ۖ قَالُوْا يٰمَرْيَمُ لَقَدْ جِئْتِ شَيْئًا فَرِيًّا ۞

28. Yaaa-'ukhta-Haaruuna maa kaana 'abuukimra-'asaw-'iñwwamaa kaanat 'um-muki bagiyyaa!

يٰٓاُخْتَ هٰرُوْنَ مَا كَانَ اَبُوْكِ امْرَاَ سَوْءٍ وَّمَا كَانَتْ اُمُّكِ بَغِيًّا ۞

29. Fa-'ashaarat 'ilayh. Qaa-luu kayfa nukallimu mañ-kaa-na fil-mahdi ṣabiyyaa?

فَاَشَارَتْ اِلَيْهِ ۖ قَالُوْا كَيْفَ نُكَلِّمُ مَنْ كَانَ فِى الْمَهْدِ صَبِيًّا ۞

30. Qaala 'innii 'Abdullaah: 'aataaniyal-Kitaaba wa ja-'ala-nii Nabiyyaa;

قَالَ اِنِّى عَبْدُ اللّٰهِ ۚ اٰتٰىنِىَ الْكِتٰبَ وَجَعَلَنِى نَبِيًّا ۞

31. Waja-'alaniimubaarakan 'ayna-maa kuntu, wa 'aw-saa-nii biṣ-Ṣalaati waz-Zakaati maa dumtu ḥayyaa:

وَّجَعَلَنِى مُبٰرَكًا اَيْنَ مَا كُنْتُ ۖ وَاَوْصٰنِى بِالصَّلٰوةِ وَالزَّكٰوةِ مَا دُمْتُ حَيًّا ۞

---

26. "So eat and drink and cool (thine) eye. And if thou dost see any man, say, 'I have vowed a fast to (Allah) Most Gracious, and this day will I enter into no talk with any human being".'

27. At length she brought the (babe) to her people, carrying him (in her arms), they said: "O Mary! truly a strange thing has thou brought!

28. "O sister of Aaron! thy father was not a man of evil, nor thy mother a woman unchaste!"

29. But she pointed to the babe. They said: "How can we talk to one who is a child in the cradle?"

30. He said: "I am indeed a servant of Allah: He hath given me revelation and made me a prophet:

31. "And He has made me blessed wheresoever I be, and hath enjoined on me prayer and zakat as long as I live;

32. Wa barram-bi-waalidatii wa lam yaj-'alnii jabbaaran shaqiyyaa;

33. Was-Salaamu 'alayya yaw-ma wulittu wa yawma 'amuutu wa yawma 'ub-'asu hayyaa!

34. Zaalika 'Iisabnu-Mar-yam: qawlal-haqqillazii fiihi yamta-ruun.

35. Maa kaana lillaahi 'any-yattakhiza minwwaladin Sub-haanah! 'Izaa qazaaa 'amran fa-'innamaa yaquulu lahuu "Kun-Fa-yakuun."

36. Wa 'innallaaha Rabbii wa Rabbukum fa-'-buduuh: haazaa Siraatum-Mustaqiim.

37. Fakhtalafal-'ahzaabu mim-baynihim: fa-waylul-lillaziina kafaruu mim-Mash-hadi yaw-min 'aziim!

38. 'Asmi' bihim wa 'absir Yawma ya'-tuunanaa laakiniz-zaalimuunal-yawma fii zalaa-lim-mubiin!

---

32. "(He hath made me) kind to my mother, and not overbearing or unblest;

33. "So Peace is on me the day I was born, the day that I die, and the day that I shall be raised up to life (again)"!

34. Such (was) Jesus the son of Mary: (it is) a statement of truth, about which they (vainly) dispute.

35. It is not befitting to (the majesty of) Allah that He should beget a son. Glory be to Him! when He determines a matter, He only says to it, "Be", and it is.

36. Verily Allah is my Lord and your Lord: Him therefore serve ye: this is a Way that is straight.

37. But the sects differ among themselves: and woe to the Unbelievers because of the (coming) Judgement of an awful Day!

38. How plainly will they see and hear, the Day that they will appear before Us! but the unjust today are in error manifest!

39. Wa'anzirhum Yawmal-Ḥasrati 'iz quẓiyal-'amr. Wa hum fii gaflatiṅwwa hum laa yu'-minuun!

40. 'Innaa Naḥnu nariṣul-'arẓa wa man 'alayhaa wa 'ilaynaa yurja-'uun. (Section 3)

41. Waẕkur fil-Kitaabi 'Ibraa-hiim: 'innahuu kaana Siddii-qan-Nabiyyaa.

42. 'Iz qaala li-'abiihi yaaa- 'abati lima ta'-budu maa laa yasma-'u wa laa yubṣiru wa laa yugnii 'anka shay-'aa?

43. Yaaa-'abati 'innii qad jaaa-'anii minal-'ilmi maa lam ya'-tika fattabi'-niii 'ahdika Ṣiraa-ṭaṅ-sawiyyaa.

44. Yaaa-'abati laa ta'- budish-Shaytaan: 'innash-Shayṭaana kaana lir-Rahmaani 'aṣiyyaa.

45. Yaaa-'abati-'inniii 'akhaa-fu 'aṅy-yamassaka 'Aẕaabum-minar-Rahmaani fatakuuna lish-Shayṭaani waliyyaa.

---

39.   But warn them of the Day of Distress, when the matter will be determined: for (behold,) they are negligent and they do"not believe!

40.   It is We Who will inherit the earth, and all beings thereon: to Us will they all be returned.

41.   (Also) mention in the Book (the story of) Abraham: he was a man of Truth, a prophet.

42.   Behold, he said to his father: "O my father! why worship that which heareth not and seeth not, and can profit thee nothing?

43.   "O my father! to me hath come knowledge which hath not reached thee: so follow me: I will guide thee to a Way that is even and straight.

44.   "O my father! serve not Satan: for Satan is a rebel against (Allah) Most Gracious.

45.   "O my father! I fear lest a Chastisement afflict thee from (Allah) Most Gracious, so that thou become to Satan a friend."

46. Qaala 'araagibun 'anta 'an 'aalihatii yaa-'Ibraahiim? La-'illam tantahi la-'arjumannaka wahjurnii maliyyaa!

47. Qaala Salaamun 'alayk: sa-'astagfiru laka Rabbii: 'in-nahuu kaana bii Ḥafiyyaa.

48. Wa 'a'-tazilukum wa maa tad-'uuna miñ duunillaahi wa 'ad-'uu Rabbii 'asaaa 'allaaa 'akuuna bi-du-'aaa-'i Rabbii shaqiyyaa.

49. Falamma'-tazalahum wa maa ya'-buduuna miñ-duunil-laahi wahabnaa lahuuu 'Is-haaqa wa Ya'-quub: wa kullan-ja-'alnaa nabiyyaa.

50. Wa wahabnaa lahum-mir-Rahmatinaa wa ja-'alnaa la-hum lisaana ṣidqin 'aliyyaa. (Section 4)

51. Wazkur fil-Kitaabi Muu-saaa 'innahuu kaana mukh-laṣañwwa kaana Rasuulan-Nabiyyaa.

---

46. (The father) replied: art thou shrinking from my gods, O Abraham? If thou forbear not, I will indeed stone thee: now get away from me for a good long while!"

47. Abraham said: "Peace be on thee: I will pray to my Lord for thy forgiveness: for He is to me Most Gracious.

48. "And I will turn away from you (all) and from those whom ye invoke besides Allah: I will call on my Lord perhaps, by my prayer to my Lord, I shall be not unblest."!

49. When he had turned away from them and from those whom they worshipped besides Allah, We bestowed on him Isaac and Jacob, and each one of them We made a prophet.

50. And We bestowed of Our Mercy on them, and We granted them lofty honour on the tongue of truth.

51. Also mention in the Book (the story of) Moses: for he was specially chosen. And he was a messenger and a prophet.

52. Wa naadaynaahu min-jaa-nibiṭ-Ṭuuril-'aymani wa qar-rabnaàhu najiyyaa.

53. Wa wahabnaa lahuu mir-Rahmatinaaa 'akhaahu Haa-ruuna Nabiyyaa.

54. Waẕkur fil-Kitaabi 'Ismaa-'iil; 'innahuu kaana ṣaadiqal-wa'-di wa kaana Rasuulan-Nabiyyaa.

55. Wa kaana ya'-muru 'ahla-huu biṣ-Ṣalaati waz-Zakaah: wa kaana 'iṅda Rabbihii mar-ẕiyyaa.

56. Waẕkur fil-Kitaabi 'Idriis: 'innahuu kaana ṣiddiiqan-Nabiyyaa:

57. Wa rafa'-naahu makaanan 'aliyyaa.

---

52. And We called him from the right side of Mount (Sinai), and made him draw near to Us, for converse in secret

53. And, out of Our Mercy, We gave him his brother Aaron, (also) a prophet.

54. Also mention in the Book (the story of) Ismā'îl: he was (strictly) true to what he promised, and he was a messenger (and) a prophet.

55. He used to enjoin on his people Prayer and zakat and he was most acceptable in the sight of his Lord.

56. Also mention in the Book Idrîs: he was a man of truth (and sincerity), (and) a prophet:

57. And We raised him to a lofty station.

58. 'Ulaaa-'ikallaẕiina 'an-'a-mallaahu 'alayhim-minan-nabiyyiina miñ-zurriyyati 'Aada-ma, wa mimman-ḥamalnaa ma-'a Nuuh, wa min zurriyyati 'Ibraahiima wa 'Israaa-'iil--wa mimman hadaynaa wajta-bay-naa. 'Iẕaa tut-laa 'alayhim 'Aayaatur-Raḥmaani kharruu sujjadañwwa bukiyyaa. (Bow-down)

59. Fa-khalafa mim-ba'-dihim khalfun 'aẕaa-'uṣ-Ṣalaata wat-taba-'ush-shahawaati fa-sawfa yalqawna gayyaa,

60. 'Illaa mañ-taaba wa 'aa-mana wa 'amila ṣaalihañ-fa-'ulaaa-'ika yadkhuluunal-Jan-nata wa laa yuẕlamuuna shay'aa,–

61. Jannaati 'Adni-nillatii wa-'adar-Raḥmaanu 'ibaadahuu bil-Gayb: 'innahuu kaana wa'-duhuu ma'-tiyyaa.

---

58. Those were some of the prophets on whom Allah did bestow His Grace,—of the posterity of Adam, and of those whom We carried (in the Ark) with Noah, and of the posterity of Abraham and Israel—of those whom We guided and chose. Whenever the Signs of (Allah) Most Gracious were rehearsed to them, they would fall down in prostrate adoration and in tears.

59. But after them there followed a posterity who missed prayers and followed after lusts soon, then, will they face Destruction,—

60. Except those who repent and believe, and work Righteousness: for these will enter the Garden and will not be wronged in the least,—

61. Gardens of Eternity, those which (Allah) Most Gracious has promised to His servants in the Unseen: for His promise must (necessarily) come to pass.

62. Laa yasma-'uuna fiihaa lagwan 'illaa Salaamaa: wa lahum rizquhum fiihaa bukra-tanwwa 'ashiyyaa.

لَا يَسْمَعُوْنَ فِيْهَا لَغْوًا اِلَّا سَلٰمًا ۚ وَلَهُمْ رِزْقُهُمْ فِيْهَا بُكْرَةً وَّعَشِيًّا ۝

63. Tilkal-Jannatullatii nuurisu min 'ibaadinaa man-kaana ta-qiyyaa.

تِلْكَ الْجَنَّةُ الَّتِىْ نُوْرِثُ مِنْ عِبَادِنَا مَنْ كَانَ تَقِيًّا ۝

64. Wa maa natanazzalu 'illaa bi-'amri Rabbik: lahuu maa bayna 'aydiinaa wa maa khalfa-naa wa maa bayna zaalik: wa maa kaana Rabbuka nasiyyaa,

وَمَا نَتَنَزَّلُ اِلَّا بِاَمْرِ رَبِّكَ ۚ لَهُ مَا بَيْنَ اَيْدِيْنَا وَمَا خَلْفَنَا وَمَا بَيْنَ ذٰلِكَ ۚ وَمَا كَانَ رَبُّكَ نَسِيًّا ۝

65. Rabbus-samaawaati wal-'arzi wa maa baynahumaa fa'-budhu wastabir li-'ibaadatih: hal ta'-lamu lahuu samiyyaa? (Section 5)

رَبُّ السَّمٰوٰتِ وَالْاَرْضِ وَمَا بَيْنَهُمَا فَاعْبُدْهُ وَاصْطَبِرْ لِعِبَادَتِهٖ ۚ هَلْ تَعْلَمُ لَهُ سَمِيًّا ۝

66. Wa yaquulul-'insaanu 'a-'izaa-maa-mittu la-sawfa 'ukhraju hayyaa?

وَيَقُوْلُ الْاِنْسَانُ ءَاِذَا مَا مِتُّ لَسَوْفَ اُخْرَجُ حَيًّا ۝

67. 'Awalaa yazkurul-'insaanu 'annaa khalaqnaahu min-qablu wa lam yaku shay-'aa?

اَوَلَا يَذْكُرُ الْاِنْسَانُ اَنَّا خَلَقْنٰهُ مِنْ قَبْلُ وَلَمْ يَكُ شَيْئًا ۝

---

62. They will not there hear any vain discourse, but only salutations of Peace: and they will have therein their sustenance, morning and evening.

63. Such is the Garden which We give as an inheritance to those of Our Servants who guard against evil.

64. (The angels say:) "We descend not but by command of thy Lord: to Him belongeth what is before us and what is behind us, and what is between: and thy Lord never doth forget,—

65. Lord of the heavens and of the earth, and of all that is between them: so worship Him, and be constant and patient in His worship: knowest thou of any who is worthy of the same Name as He?

66. Man says: "What! when I am dead, shall I then be raised up alive?"

67. But does not man call to mind that We created him before out of nothing?

68. Fawa Rabbika lanah-shu-rannahum wash-shayaatiina summa la-nuhzi-rannahum hawla Jahannama jisiyyaa;

69. Summa lananzi-'anna min kulli shii-'atin 'ayyuhum 'ashaddu 'alar-Rahmaani 'itiyyaa.

70. Summa la-nahnu 'a'-lamu billaziina hum 'awlaa bihaa siliyyaa.

71. Wa 'imminkum 'illaa waa-riduhaa: kaana 'alaa Rabbika Hatmam-maqziyyaa.

72. Summa nunajjil-laziinatta-qaw-wa nazaruz-zaalimiina fiihaa jisiyyaa.

73. Wa 'izaa tutlaa 'alayhim 'Aayaatunaa bayyinaatin-qaa-lallaziina kafaruu lillaziina 'aamanuuu 'ayyul-fariiqayni khayrum-Maqaamanwwa 'ah-sanu Nadiyyaa?

---

68. So, by thy Lord, without doubt, We shall gather them together, and (also) Satans (with them); then shall We bring them forth on their knees round about Hell;

69. Then shall We certainly drag out from every sect all those who were worst in obstinate rebellion against (Allah) Most Gracious.

70. And certainly We know best those who are most worthy of being burned therein.

71. Not one of you but will pass over it: this is, with thy Lord, a Decree which must be accomplished.

72. But We shall save those who guarded against evil, and We shall leave the wrong-doers therein, (humbled) to their knees.

73. When Our Clear Signs are rehearsed to them, the Unbelievers say to those who believe, "Which of the two sides is best in point of position and fairer in assembly,"

74. Wa kam 'ahlaknaa qabla-hum-min-qarnin hum 'ahsanu 'asaasanwwa ri'-yaa?

75. Qul man-kaana fizzalaala-ti falyamdud lahur-Rahmaanu maddaa: hattaaa 'izaa ra-'aw maa yuu-'aduuna 'immal-'azaaba wa 'immas-Saa-'ah. Fasaya'-lamuuna man huwa sharrum-makaananwwa 'az-'afu jundaa!

76. Wa yaziidul-laahul-lazii-nahtadaw Hudaa; wal-Baaqi-yaatus-Saalihaatu khayrun 'inda Rabbika sawaabanwwa khayrum-maraddaa.

77. 'Afara-'aytallazii kafara bi-'Aayaatinaa wa qaala la-'uutayanna maalanwwa wala-daa?

78. 'Attala-'al-Gayba 'amitta-khaza 'indar-Rahmaani 'ahdaa?

---

74. But how many (countless) generations before them have We destroyed, who were even better in equipment and in glitter to the eye?

75. Say: "Whoever goes astray, (Allah) Most Gracious extends (the rope) to them, until, when they see the warning of Allah (being fulfilled)—either in punishment or in (the approach of) the Hour,—they will at length realise who is worst in position, and (who) weakest in forces!

76. "And Allah doth increase in guidance those who seek guidance: and the things that endure, Good Deeds, are best in the sight of thy Lord, as rewards, and best in respect of (their) eventual returns."

77. Has thou then seen the (sort of) man who rejects Our Signs, yet says: "I shall certainly be given wealth and children?"

78. Has he penetrated to the Unseen, or has he taken a promise with the Most Gracious?

79. Kallaa! Sanaktubu maa yaquulu wa namuddu lahuu minal-'azaabi maddaa.

80. Wa narisuhuu maa yaquu-lu wa ya'tiinaa fardaa.

81. Wattakhazuu min-duunil-laahi 'aalihatal-liyakuunuu la-hum-'izzaa!

82. Kallaa! sayakfuruuna bi-'ibaadatihim wa yakuunuuna 'alayhim ziddaa. (Section 6)

83. 'Alam tara 'annaaa 'arsal-nash-shayaatiina 'alal-kaafiriina ta-'uzzuhum 'azzaa?

84. Falaa ta'-jal 'alayhim: 'innamaa na-'uddu lahum 'addaa.

85. Yawma nah-shurul-Mutta-qiina 'ilar-Rahmaani wafdaa,

86. Wa nasuuqul-mujrimiina 'ilaa Jahannama wirdaa.

87. Laa yamlikuunash-shafaa-'ata 'illaa manittakhaza 'indar-Rahmaani 'ahdaa.

---

79. Nay! We shall record what he says, and We shall add and add to his punishment.

80. To Us shall return all that he talks of, and he shall appear before Us bare and alone.

81. And they have taken (for worship) gods other than Allah, to give them power and glory!

82. Instead, they shall reject their worship, and become adversaries against them.

83. Seest thou not that We have set Satans on against the Unbelievers, to incite them with fury?

84. So make no haste against them, for We but count out to them a (limited) number (of days).

85. The day We shall gather the righteous to (Allah) Most Gracious, like a band (presented before a king for honours.)

86. And We shall drive the sinners to hell, (like thirsty cattle driven down to water,—)

87. None shall have the power of intercession, but such a one as has received permission (or promise) from (Allah) Most Gracious.

88.　Wa qaaluttakhazar-Rah-maanu waladaa!

وَقَالُوا اتَّخَذَ الرَّحْمٰنُ وَلَدًا ۝

89.　Laqad ji'-tum shay-'an 'iddaa!

لَقَدْ جِئْتُمْ شَيْئًا إِدًّا ۝

90.　Takaadus-samaawaatu ya-tafattarna minhu wa tanshaq-qul-'arzu wa takhirrul-jibaalu haddaaa,

تَكَادُ السَّمٰوٰتُ يَتَفَطَّرْنَ مِنْهُ وَتَنْشَقُّ الْأَرْضُ وَتَخِرُّ الْجِبَالُ هَدًّا ۝

91.　'An-da-'aw lir-Rahmaani waladaa.

أَنْ دَعَوْا لِلرَّحْمٰنِ وَلَدًا ۝

92.　Wa maa yambagii lir-Rahmaani 'any-yattakhiza waladaa.

وَمَا يَنْبَغِي لِلرَّحْمٰنِ أَنْ يَتَّخِذَ وَلَدًا ۝

93.　'In-kullu man-fis-samaa-waati wal-'arzi 'illaaa 'aatir-Rahmaani 'abdaa.

إِنْ كُلُّ مَنْ فِي السَّمٰوٰتِ وَالْأَرْضِ إِلَّا آتِي الرَّحْمٰنِ عَبْدًا ۝

94.　Laqad 'ah-saahum wa 'ad-dahum 'addaa.

لَقَدْ أَحْصَاهُمْ وَعَدَّهُمْ عَدًّا ۝

95.　Wa kulluhum 'aatiihi yawmal-Qiyaamati fardaa.

وَكُلُّهُمْ آتِيهِ يَوْمَ الْقِيٰمَةِ فَرْدًا ۝

88.　They say: "The Most Gracious has betaken a son!"

89.　Indeed ye have put forth a thing most monstrous!

90.　At it the skies are about to burst, the earth to split asunder, and the mountains to fall down in utter ruin,

91.　That they attributed a son to the Most Gracious.

92.　For it is not consonant with the majesty of the Most Gracious that He should beget a son.

93.　Not one of the beings in the heavens and the earth but must come to the Most Gracious as a servant.

94.　He does take an account of them (all), and hath numbered them (all) exactly.

95.　And everyone of them will come to Him singly on the Day of Judgement.

96.   'Innallaziina 'aamanuu wa ' a milus-saalihaati sayaj-'alu lahumur-Rahmaanu wuddaa.

إِنَّ الَّذِيْنَ اٰمَنُوْا وَعَمِلُوا الصّٰلِحٰتِ سَيَجْعَلُ لَهُمُ الرَّحْمٰنُ وُدًّا ۝

97.   Fa-'innamaa yassarnaahu bi-lisaanika li-tubash-shira bi-hil-Muttaqiina wa tunzira bi-hii qawmal-luddaa.

فَإِنَّمَا يَسَّرْنٰهُ بِلِسَانِكَ لِتُبَشِّرَ بِهِ الْمُتَّقِيْنَ وَتُنْذِرَ بِهِ قَوْمًا لُّدًّا ۝

98.   Wa kam 'ahlaknaa qabla-hum-min-qarn? Hal tuhissu minhum-min-'ahadin 'aw tas-ma-'u lahum rikzaa? (Part One-half)

وَكَمْ أَهْلَكْنَا قَبْلَهُمْ مِّنْ قَرْنٍ هَلْ تُحِسُّ مِنْهُمْ مِّنْ أَحَدٍ أَوْ تَسْمَعُ لَهُمْ رِكْزًا ۝

---

96.   On those who believe and work deeds of righteousness, will the Most Gracious bestow Love.

97.   So have We made the (Qur-ān) easy in thine own tongue, that with it thou mayest give glad tidings to the righteous, and warnings to people given to contention.

98.   But how many (countless) generations before them have We destroyed? Canst thou find a single one of them (now) or hear (so much as) a whisper of them?

Taariq–86
Verses 17–Section 1

بِسْمِ اللهِ الرَّحْمٰنِ الرَّحِيْمِ ۝

Bismillaahir-Raḥmaanir-Raḥiim.

1. Was-Samaaa-'i wat-ṬAARIQ;

وَالسَّمَآءِ وَالطَّارِقِ ۝

2. Wa maaa 'adraaka mat-Taariq?

وَمَآ أَدْرٰىكَ مَا الطَّارِقُ ۝

3. 'An-Najmuṣ-ṣaaqib!

النَّجْمُ الثَّاقِبُ ۝

4. 'In-kullu nafsil-lammaa 'alayhaa ḥaafiẓ.

إِنْ كُلُّ نَفْسٍ لَّمَّا عَلَيْهَا حَافِظٌ ۝

5. Fal-yañẓuril-'insaanu-mimma khuliq.

فَلْيَنْظُرِ الْإِنْسَانُ مِمَّ خُلِقَ ۝

6. Khuliqa mimmaaa-'iñdaa-fiq,

خُلِقَ مِنْ مَّآءٍ دَافِقٍ ۝

7. Yakhruju mim-bayniṣ-ṣulbi wat-taraaa-'ib.

يَخْرُجُ مِنْ بَيْنِ الصُّلْبِ وَالتَّرَآئِبِ ۝

8. 'Inna-Huu 'alaa raj-'ihii la-qaadir.

إِنَّهُ عَلٰى رَجْعِهِ لَقَادِرٌ ۝

At-Tāriq, or The Night-Visitant

In the name of Allah, Most Gracious, Most Merciful.

1. By the Sky and the Night-Visitant (therein);
2. And what will explain to thee what the Night-Visitant is?—
3. (It is) the Star of piercing brightness;—
4. There is no soul but has a protector over it.
5. Now let man but think from what he is created !
6. He is created from a drop emitted—
7. Proceeding from between the backbone and the ribs:
8. Surely (Allah) is able to bring him back (to life) !

9. Yawma tublas-saraaa-'ir,

10. Famaa lahuu min-quw-watinw-wa laa naasir.

11. Was-Samaaa-'i zaatir-raj',

12. Wal-'arzi zaatis-sad',—

13. 'Innahuu la-qawlun-fasl:

14. Wa maa huwa bil-hazl.

15. 'Innahum yakiiduuna kaydaa,

16. Wa 'akiidu kaydaa.

17. Fa-mahhilil-kaafiriina 'amhilhum ru-waydaa.

---

9. The Day that (all) things secret will be tested,
10. (Man) will have no power, and no helper.
11. By the Firmament which giveth the returning rain,
12. And by the Earth which opens out (for the gushing of springs or the sprouting of vegetation),—
13. Behold this is the Word that distinguishes (Good from Evil):
14. It is not a thing for amusement.
15. As for them, they are but plotting a scheme,
16. And I am planning a scheme.
17. Therefore grant a delay to the Unbelievers: give respite to them gently (for awhile).

Faatihah—1

Verses 7 — Section 1

Bismillaahir-Raḥmaanir-Raḥiim.

1. 'Al-Ḥamdu lillaahi Rabbil-'Aalamiin;

2. 'Ar-Raḥmaanir-Rahiim;

3. Maaliki Yawmid-Diin!

4. 'Iyyaaka na'-budu wa 'iyyaaka nasta-'iin.

5. 'Ihdinaṣ-Ṣiraaṭal-Musta-qiim—

6. Ṣiraaṭal-laẕiina 'an-'amta 'alay-him—

7. Gayril-magẕuubi 'alay-him wa laẕ-ẕaaalliin.

Al-Fātîha, or the Opening Chapter

1. In the name of Allah, Most Gracious, Most Merciful.
2. Praise be to Allah, the Cherisher and Sustainer of the Worlds:
3. Most Gracious, Most Merciful;
4. Master of the Day of Judgement.
5. Thee do we worship, and Thine aid we seek.
6. Show us the straight way,
7. The way of those on whom Thou has bestowed Thy Grace, those whose (portion) is not wrath. And who go not astray.

Kaafiruun–109
Verses 6–Section 1

Bismillaahir-Rahmaanir-Rahiim.

1. Qul yaaa-'ayyuhal-KAAFIRUUN!

2. Laaa 'a'-budu maa ta'-bu-duun,

3. Wa laaa 'antum 'aabiduuna maaa 'a'-bud.

4. Wa laaa 'ana 'aabidum-maa 'abattum,

5. Wa laaa 'antum 'aabiduuna maaa 'a'-bud.

6. Lakum Diinukum wa li-ya Diin.

Al-Kāfirûn, or Those Who Reject Faith

In the name of Allah, Most Gracious, Most Merciful.

1. Say: O ye that reject Faith !
2. I worship not that which ye worship,
3. Nor will ye worship that which I worship.
4. And I will not worship that which ye have been wont to worship
5. Nor will ye worship that which I worship.
6. To you be your Way, and to me mine.

'Ikhlaas–112
Verses 4–Section 1

Bismillaahir-Rahmaanir-Rahiim.

1. Qul Hu-wallaahu 'Ahad;

2. 'Allaahus-Samad;

3. Lam yalid, wa lam yuulad;

4. Walam yakul-la-Huu kufuwan 'ahad.

Al-Ikhlās, or Purity (of Faith)

In the name of Allah, Most Gracious, Most Merciful.

1. Say: He is Allah the One;
2. Allah, the Eternal, Absolute;
3. He begetteth not, nor is He begotten;
4. And there is none like unto Him.

Falaq–113
Verses 5–Section 1

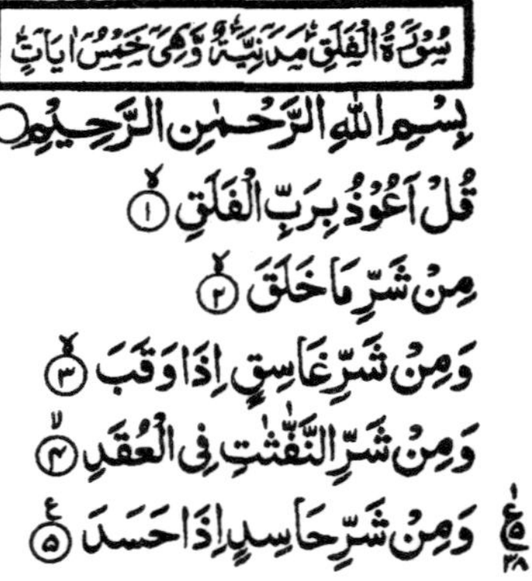

Bismillaahir-Rahmaanir-Rahiim.

1. Qul 'a-'uuzu bi-Rabbil-Falaq,

2. Miñ-sharri maa khalaq:

3. Wa miñ-sharri gaasiqin 'izaa waqab,
4. Wa miñ-sharrin-Naffaasaati fil-'uqad,
5. Wa miñ-sharri haasidin 'izaa hasad.

Al-Falaq, or The Dawn

In the name of Allah, Most Gracious, Most Merciful.

1. Say: I seek refuge with the Lord of the Dawn,
2. From the mischief of created things;
3. From the mischief of Darkness as it overspreads;
4. From the mischief of those who blow on knots;
5. And from the mischief of the envious one as he practises envy.

Naas–114
Verses 6–Section 1

Bismillaahir-Rahmaanir-Rahiim.

1. Qul 'a-'uuzu bi-Rabbin-NAAS.
2. Malikin-Naas,
3. 'Ilaahin-Naas.
4. Min-sharril-Waswaasil-khan-Naas,–
5. 'Allazii yuwas-wisu fii suduurin-Naasi,–
6. Minal-Jinnati wan-Naas.

An-Nãs, or Mankind

In the name of Allah, Most Gracious, Most Merciful.

1. Say: I seek refuge with the Lord and Cherisher of Mankind,
2. The King (or Ruler) of Mankind,
3. The God (or Judge) of Mankind,—
4. From the mischief of the Whisperer (of Evil), who withdraws (after his whisper),—
5. Who whispers into the hearts of Mankind,—
6. Among Jinns and among Men.